HIGHER EDUCATION IN ARUNACHAL PRADESH

HIGHER EDUCATION IN ARUNACHAL PRADESH

P.K. NAYAK

AKANSHA PUBLISHING HOUSE
NEW DELHI - 110 059 (INDIA)

Akansha Publishing House
R 37-B, Vani Vihar, Uttam Nagar
New Delhi - 110 059
E-mail: ektabooks@yahoo.com

Higher Education in Arunachal Pradesh

First Edition, 2002

ISBN 81-87606-15-0

PRINTED IN INDIA

Published by M.P. Misra for Akansha Publishing House, New Delhi - 110 059 and Printed at Mehra Offset Press, Delhi.

CONTENTS

	Preface	*vii*
	Abbreviations	*xi*
1.	Introduction	1
2.	Education: Props for Development	15
3.	Dynamics of Teaching and Testing	52
4.	Arunachal Pradesh: An Overview of Its Education System	79
5.	The District: West Kameng	128
6.	The Problem and the Critical Eye	174
7.	Epilogue	204
	Appendix	227
	Bibliography	238
	Index	243

PREFACE

In a country like India where variety marks physical, social, economic and cultural aspects, any worthwhile attempt at understanding the way education operates at the national level must endeavour to deal with variations peculiar to local contexts. The global nature of the national level study excludes the peculiarities of the particular regions. For instance, national figures regarding enrolment, dropout, number of schools in states and such other indicators of educational growth would only minimally explain the actual support or constraints education faces in different regions. Also certain other indicators such as number of teachers, infrastructural facilities available etc. alongwith information on perceptions of people, problems faced, reactions of teachers, general receptivity for the new things in the local cultural context are felt to be useful assessing the effectiveness of education provided in any area/region. Besides, other features of relevance would be consideration of locations of villages, nature of economic activities carried on and the socio-cultural functions. Studying such varied details can make national level observations meaningful. Hence, the need of studying a smaller unit, such as a district or a village or a community with distinct socio-cultural identity.

The present investigation is an attempt to carry out a research and survey of one such smaller phenomenon, viz. need for higher education in the West Kameng district of Arunachal Pradesh, basically stressing upon the dropouts.

In attempting such a research the present study focuses on the various aspects related to education—primary, secondary and higher in the said district, causes of dropouts at different stages of education accounting for the very slow process of enrolment for higher education extent, of utilisation of educational facilities, perception of parents and local people regarding education, the way education has influenced the people of different subgroups in the rural setup, any possible improvement qualitatively, the extent of utilisation of development programmes launched by state government and such other related aspects.

Main objectives behind this study of the district have been to examine the socio-economic status (SES) of the family of a student dropping out on the way, i.e. failures in different classes to reach higher education, to identify the cases whether rising out of first generation education to analyse the problem arising out of the ineffective teaching methods or due to the pattern of education prevalent at the elementary and secondary levels; to focus the study of different aspects like administration, organisation, evaluation and inspection, teacher and research practices etc. contributing to the aggravation of the problem; and to make circlewise survey of all the school facilities presently made available in the district.

The study has been based basically on primary, secondary and tertiary sources, i.e. the official records in the departmental files, committe reports, bounding survey publications, published books, monographs and other printed materials at the state, district, circle, village and institutional level. For the collection of data the offices of the Deputy Director of School Education (DDSE)), West Kameng, district, Bomdila and the Director of School Education (DSE), Naharlagun have been consulted. The said offices have greatly come to the use for gathering informations regarding the existing schools, infrastructure, enrolment, dropouts, teaching strength etc. Moreover, three types of questionnaires, Family Based, Student Based and Teacher Based, were prepared and used for collecting data for analysing various aspects of the problem of the students going for dropouts.

I am indebted to the University Grants Commision, NER Office, Guwahati for funding me this Minor Research Project on "Need for Higher Education in Arunachal Pradesh: A Case Study of West Kameng District" and to the Arunachal University, Itanagar for forwarding my proposal for MRP to the UGC without which the project would not have been a reality.

The study is an outcome of the collaborative help and cooperation of the NIEPA, NCERT and Ministry of HRD, New Delhi; the Director of School Education, Naharlagan; the Principal, Government College, Bomdila; the DDSE, West Kameng District, Bomdila that they rendered me for the collection of relevant informations. My compliments are there with the whole team of personnel at district, circle, village and institutional levels for their active cooperation during my field study. I am grateful to Sri P. Jayaraman, ADEO, Office of the DDSE, Bomdila, K.C. Mishra, Teacher, Karangania Primary School (Thrizino Circle), S.D. Pandey, M.M. Nayak, A.K. Shandilya, Sanjay Tyagi, M.B. Singh, all teachers in the different circles; Sri P.T. Dhingla, R.D. Thungon, Yese Gyesen, Passang Tsering, Tenzin Sagro, all students-cum-guides for their incredible help but for which this work would not have completed.

I owe a deep debt of gratitude to Sri Arun Baroka, IAS, DC, West Kameng District for allowing me to get my project-related accounts audited by Sri E.S. Skariah, Inspecting Auditor, DC Office, Bomdila. I am obliged to Sri Skariah too.

My sincere gratitude is due to Prof. S.P. Pani, Director, DDCE, Utkal University, Bhubaneswar, Orissa and Mrs. Uma Dutta, Principal, Government College, Bomdila who have been the constant sources of inspiration all through the days for the successful completion of the work. I am highly obliged to Dr. K.C. Mishra, Senior Lecturer in English, Government College, Bomdila for his expert guidance and valuable suggestions at various stages of the study; to Sri D.K. Mishra, Lecturer, Department of Economics, Arunachal University, Itanagar and Dr. M. Sharma, Lecturer in Economics of my college for their selfless help; to Miss Diptimayee Dalai and Sabita Mallik, DDCE, Utkal University, Bhubaneswar and Wange's Computer World, Bomdila for word processing the work in the computer and also to a number of other persons for rendering me either direct or indirect help whenever needed.

My wife Reenee and daughter Prachi Mrdula (Himani) take away the best of my success. Daughter's oftern stormy and rigid kind of disturbances during the preparation of the report were the lovely scintillating moments asking me to put my abiding interest to go further.

Hopefully, this report will throw new light on the educational setup of the study area and ask the planners and researchers to undertake research for further development of education in the state.

Government College
Bomdila, West Kameng,
Arunachal Pradesh-790 001

P.K. Nayak

ABBREVIATIONS

ADAEO—Assistant District Adult Education Officer.

ADEO—Assistant District Education Officer.

AEO—Adult Education Officer.

AES—Adult Education Supervisor

AIES—All India Educational Survey.

AISSCE—All India Senior School Certificate Examination.

AISSE—All India Secondary School Examination.

APCS—Arunachal Pradesh Civil Service.

AT—Assistant Teacher.

BSB—Basic Shiksha Bhawan.

CAI—Computer Assisted Instruction.

CAL—Computer Aided Learning.

CBSE—Central Board of Secondary Education.

CEO—Chief Education Officer.

CET—Centre for Educational Technology.

CIEFL—Central Institute of English and Foreign Languages.

CIET—Central Institute of Educational Technology.

CLASS—Computer Literacy and Studies in Schools.

CTE—College of Teacher Education.

DAEO—District Adult Education Officer.

DDSE—Deputy Director of School Education

DIET—District Institute of Education and Training.

DSE—Director of School Education.

DRCSE—District Resource Centre for Science Education.

ECCE—Early Childhood Care and Education.

EFA—Education For All.

JT—Junior Teacher.

MHRD—Ministry of Human Resource Development.

NCERT—National Council of Educational Research and Training.

NCTE—National Council of Teacher Education.

NEC—North Eastern Council.

NEFA—North Eastern Frontier Agnecy.

NERIST—North Eastern Region Institute of Science and Technology.

NIEPA—National Institute of Educational Planning and Administration.

NPE—National Policy on Education.

OB—Operation Blackboard.

PMOST—Programme of Mass Orientation of School Teachers.

POA—Programme of Action.

RLEGP—Rural Labour Employment Generation Programme.

SCERT—State Council of Educational Research and Training.

SIE—State Institute of Education.

SIET—State Institute of Educational Training.

SRC—State Resource Centre.

SUPW—Social Useful Productive Work.

ST—Senior Teacher.

UEE—Universalisation of Elementary Education.

1

INTRODUCTION

Man has tried across the span of human life on earth, within the limitations of his potentialities to make adjustments to the physical universe and to the social world about him. This process of adjustment has endeared him before his environment and social worlds, thereby creating in him a tinge for cultural integrity. Endowment of certain qualities such as easy manipulation of hands and of use of speech make him a highly expressive and creative being. His magic, religion, art, literature and the rest of the world of symbols are as much instrumentalities of his adjustive process as his material tools, architecture and technologies inventions. He creates these instrumentalities in order to feel at home, although it is another matter that having created them he loses rather complete mastery over them and in turn, may be slaved by them. This process again calls for renewed effort to adjustment and balance and so the gamut of change goes on.

Social change at its source is just a part of this broad based biological-psychological process. True, on the basis of anthropological and archaeological studies that society has never been absolutely static. In the early history of man's life change has of course been dead slow as in the vast eras of the Ice Ages. But albeit man's innovations in the fields of tool-making and agriculture have been galvanizing the process of change until today when the world is snared in the whirlpool of technological and social changes.

Although social change is a stubborn fact of human life, yet not all social change is good in its own right. It is for this reason that EDUCATION, as a tool of social control, has to perform two interpersed functions : one to assimilate, preserve and transmit the useful elements of the cultural patterns throbbing with the new vitalities of people and answering the list of social values. Hence, education, as a highly organised institution of society, must negotiate cultural heritage with open eyes and creative zeal. While assimilating and transmitting cultural heritage it must question as well as experiment and in that light modify it. The dynamic and durable culture is the one that keeps on admitting new change and new influences without losing its own moorings and cardinal human values. The school as a considerable partner of society, but with its own privileges of independence must exercise all its resources to achieve the aforesaid objectives in the most thoughtful and creative way.

There is a sensitive objection that the modern school is not well coping the responsibility of conserving the best of the cultural heritage and is hypnotically giving in to anything new and tantalizing. That needs a serious investigation in the best ways of research on the part of every educational institution so that the hard earned solid gains of the past are not simply thrown away with or without any social acquisitions from the new elements of life. Whether or not the objection be valid, it surely puts the school in its proper sphere of responsibility. The inescapable task of the school, and more so of the universities is to keep the emerging cultural patterns always under review and research so that under the guise of modernity no debilitating elements creep into the mainstream of life. The departments of sociology, psychology and philosophy of the universities need carry out a co-ordinated plan of research on this vital issue on which rests the very fate of civilization.

Hence education has always been linked to life and society. Since education is a sub-system of society, societal vision and priorities will necessarily be reflected in education. While the pace of change has been slow in the past, that is no more true in the present context. The changes are of such a nature and occur with such rapidity that many persons go into a state of shock as a result. It is, therefore, imperative that necessary changes are made in the educational process so as to enable individuals and the society to cope with the change.

That knowledge is power, perceived a long time ago has been most forcefully demonstrated by the developed countries. It is not iron and coal, not oil nor even the accumulation of wealth that has made a few nations very rich and powerful, but the relentless pursuit of knowledge and its myriad applications through technology. Those nations which possess a high degree of knowledge and which have developed the ability to create new knowledge and thus have acquired power over nature, by understanding its laws, that have been inventing newer and newer technologies. Knowledge and technology have made it possible to acquire vast amounts of wealth. The power that has become available through knowledge, technology and money to the developing nations, has also made the developing nations remain at the receiving end.

The Essence and Role of Education

Almost universally, education, is seen as an instrument that will positively and effectively contribute to making a better world. This is based on the fact that education has a definite role in developing the quality of minds of the people, the temper of their hearts and attitudes and the skills of their hands. Developing that boundless resource, the Human Person is therefore, also closely linked with national development. Education, as it is hoped, needs to produce a new person.

Education basically suffers from the gap between its context and the living experience of its pupils, between the system of values that it preaches and the goals set up by society, between its ancient curricular and the modernity of science. Linking education to life, associating it with concrete goals, establishing a close relationship between society and economy, inventing or rediscovering an education system fitting its surroundings, surely brings about multi-dimensional solutions to the problems mankind forces (Inderpal Singh: 75).

For far too long, education had the task of preparing for stereotyped functions, stable situations, for one moment in existence, for a particular trade or a given job. It inculcated conventional knowledge in time honoured categories. This concept is still far too prevalent. And yet, the idea of acquiring, at an early age, a set of intellectual or technical equipment that is valid for a life time is out of date. This fundamental axiom of traditional education is tottering. Is not this the time to call for something quite different in education system? Learning to live, learning to learn, so as to be able to absorb new knowledge all through life, learning to think forcefully and critically, learning to love the world and make it more human, learning to develop in and through creative work.

Seemingly abstract words. But education is such a big undertaking, it has so radical an influence on man's destiny that it will be damaging if it is only considered in terms of structures, logistical means and process. The very substance of education, its essential relationship to man and his development, its interaction with the environment, as both product and factor of society, must all be deeply scrutinised and expensively reconsidered.

Like every other human enterprise, education also follows the law of growing old and therefore, gathering increasing amount of irrelevance. To remain alive education must constantly question its objectives, its content, and its methods.

From one view point aims of education may be taken as universal or particular. Universal aims are those which apply in their generality to all mankind. Developing human qualities such as love and non-violence are or anything to be, universal aims of education. Integration of human personality, sound physical and mental health, in keeping with the maximum of the health and progress of society are as well the universal aims of education. There are certain fundamentals in the life of individual and society, like fundamentals in any other field; which give education on one plane, a universal character. All sound philosophies and educational theories are agreed on this no matter what their language be. The intrinsic values are universal.

Individual or particular aims are limited in scope and character. They are related to times and conditions. They are also a matter of emphasis following certain exigencies. For example, a technologically backward country may of necessity emphasise, out of proportions, the place of science and technology in the curriculum. That does not mean that the values of science and technology are superior in merit to the basic human values. All it means is that to promote the human values it is necessary in particular conditions of a society to give top priority to technical subjects so that adequate material progress is assured. But if the material and technology become the vanguard in the march leaving human values in the rear there is serious reason for the educationists to feel alarmed. The particular aims, however good and useful, should not defy the universal, intrinsic aims of education, rather on the other hand enrich them.

It is one of the major tasks of education to keep the two in proper harmony for generally what happens is that the universal aims are constantly harped upon without due regard to the specific situations calling for specific curriculum and specific methods of education, or the specific problems are addressed to in a limited way in other disregard to the intrinsic universal values. Thus, to take an instance, if India in the very early phase of educational reconstruction were to gear the whole system of education to attain spiritual ends at the cost of technological progress she might end up spiritually bankrupt and without adding anything to her material wealth. Or the other way round, if she were to insist on the progress of the technological knowledge at any cost without any heed to her spiritual heritage she would still be committing an educational folly.

Particular aims of education, which are in the nature of extrinsic or instrumental values – values whose function is to realise higher or instrinsic values have their justification so long as they do not contradict the basic values. The aims of education, therefore, is the extent of harmony and balance to be found in universal and particular aims.

Education is widely accepted as necessary tool for attainment of developmental goals. The role of education in development is related with its three major functions, viz. literacy, information diffusion and skill inculcation. It is quite clear that taken together these three functions constitute the main contribution of education on the development all over the world. The movement for a mass based education system in USA and Canada in the nineteenth century partly owes itself to this aspect. It arrived in the wake of mass industrial development. This is markedly different from that of the growth of education in UK and other European countries. Education played only a minor role in the initial stages of industrial revolution in these countries. It is only towards the later end of industrial revolution that it became imperative to spread education in UK and Europe, to facilitate the further economic growth.

The role of education in the modern period hardly needs any advocacy. But the problem is that when the poorer nations are launching their plans, given the nature of contemporary development, they are obliged to fulfil the precondition of education. They are not attempting to finish crawl and the run, but to run straight way, because in the present times it is the nature of available technology and innovations which governs development. These countries have to move straight from pre-industrial age to modern pre-industrial stage, in these countries, the pressures on education, to facilitate this process, are tremendous. Their educational system has to deliver in as timing range of output to match the varying requirements of modern development. Educational system is not only to impart education but also so many other services get facilitated by its process. The institutions of educational system become conduct for many other inputs, like creation, health and community services. The growth of educational institutions should act as a facilitator for all such services.

In addition, the curriculum also becomes an important means of inculcating appropriate social values in the students. Such curriculum helps in forging together an identity in society. It also helps in developing common ethos of social members by inter-mixing the children from different socio-economic families together. In India, where due to lack of infrastructural facilities, the interior areas are aloof from the rest of the society, the spread of educational system is all the more important. Similarly, for creating a mutually accommodating climate in caste and class ridden villages it has an important role to play. It is in this sense, the objective of education is stated to be, education for development of manpower (B.L. Raina: 26-27).

Education can not be considered in isolation but should be related to other sectors of development. In this connection, the General Conference of UNESCO affirmed that by the very complexity of the problems which it must help to solve, education must be concerned in an inter-disciplinary context as a factor of multidimensional development of which man is both the end and the instrument (J.P. Naik: 1978). Education has three important interrelated functions. First as a basic human need, people need education to acquire a broad spectrum of knowledge, attitudes, value and skills which they can develop later on. Secondly, as a means of meeting other needs, education influences and is in turn influenced by access to the other basic needs like adequate nutrition, safe drinking water, health services and shelter. Third, as an activity, that sustains and accelerates over all development as a consequence of trained manpower development to manage capital technology, services and administration in every sector of economy.

However, education is rendered limited by mainly the prevailing economic order, political power and social structure. Inspite of various advances made in this sphere and the wider spread of education, there is inequality in terms of its distribution among different social strata. Further, one-third of the children in the primary age group are not enrolled in schools, 60 per cent drop out before reaching the fifth standard, another 15 per cent before reaching eighth. Only half the number complete the school certificate examination (Raina: 29-30). The situation is more alarming in the case of weaker sections of society, especially the backward classes and scheduled castes and tribes, where poverty, low social and political status and cultural deprivation are dominant. The literacy in India has been improving considerably. After Independence it has increased from 16.67 per cent in 1951 to 43.4 per cent in 1981, and 52.1 per cent in 1991, 24.95 per cent (males) and 7.93 per cent (females) in 1951 to 56.4 per cent (males) and 29.8 per cent (females) in 1981 and 63.9 per cent (males) and female 39.4 per cent in 1991.

The growth of literacy rate by 8.5 per cent during 1981-91 decade, marks a slight progress over 7 per cent of the 1971-81 decade. If the country moves at this rate, it is expected that it can achieve total literacy by 2040. But female literacy is still very discouraging-the larger percentage being contributed by the BIMARU States, Bihar, Madhya Pradesh,

Rajasthan and Uttar Pradesh. The total female literacy is expected by 2060. The World Bank has estimated that India will have 500 million illustrates by 2000—constituting 54 per cent of the world's illiterate population. This is quite alarming for a democratic country like India. It is against such an intensely intimidating scenario that study of drop outs case assumes special significance. Also it appears quite inevitable to arrest the dropouts problems or else compounded with the illiteracy position, a greater challenge will emerge which will out race all our efforts to attain the EFA (Education for All) goal.

However, it is encouraging to note that there has been a steady in course in literacy, but this has uneven sexwise and regionwise distribution. Apart from the problem of having access to opportunities of education, the better educational facilities are also concentrated in the urban areas. In order to have equalitarian pattern of development in a democratic set-up like ours, it is important to have a balanced growth of education in the rural and urban areas.

In this regard, it needs to be recognised that such imbalances or variations in the very functioning of education in different areas are caused by factors and processes outside education. In other words, the ground procedures adopted at the national level and state level are similar all over. But a lot of variations will be there in the extent to which these operate effectively, depending on the local socio-cultural environment.

More precisely the aim of education is to help students develop their critical faculties, their capacities for thinking and judging and for modifying their behaviour so that now and later their education does not fail them to evaluate the life situations correctly and deal with them and promptly. The pragmatic educationists aim to develop the social intelligence of children has a substantial relevance in this context. Further, education succeeds in its aim to the degree it is able to make it acceptable to the pupils that learning in life is not entirely in the gift of the school master but something to be won by their own efforts, maybe with more or less aid of the society, school and the teacher who serve as noble instrumentalities for the harmonious development of the former. Education in its aim emerges, by a little emphasis, to be a case of self-education. The test of the progress of any educational institution is as to how far it has made its principles fit for the career of self-education (Prem Nath: 92).

The aim of education as such turns out to be the total education of the whole individual for the total and wholesome life through mainly self-effort in the atmosphere with the community.

In a country like India, which is full of variety in physical, social, economic and cultural aspects any attempt at understanding the way education operate at a national level provides a very global view which is too comprehensive and complex to reflect such variations peculiar to local contexts. Hence, data attempted at the national level excludes the peculiarities of the particular regions. In an attempt to evolve a common view regarding the entire nation, they reveal only the generalities but not peculiarities specific to local regions. For instance, national figures regarding enrolment, dropout, number of schools in states and such other indicators of educational growth would only minimally explain the actual support constraints education faces in different regions. Such information is very much necessary. Also required are certain other indicators such as number of teachers, infrastructure facilities available as quantitative informations at grass root level alongwith qualitative information such as perceptions of people, problem faced reactions of teachers, general receptivity for the new things in the local cultural context. Besides, other features of relevance would be in the form of the locations or village nearer to city, nature of economic activities carried on and the socio-cultural functions. Studying such varied details at a national level is to difficult but meaningful. Hence, the need of studying a smaller unit, such as a district or a village or a community with distinct socio-cultural identity is very much essential.

The present investigation is an attempt to carry out a research and survey of one such smaller phenomenon, viz. need for higher education in the West Kameng District of Arunachal Pradesh basically stressing upon the drop outs. In attempting such a research the present study focuses on the various aspects related to education-primary, secondary and higher in the said district, causes of drop outs at different stages of education accounting for the very slow process of enrolment for higher education, extent of utilization of educational facilities, perceptions of parents and local people regarding education, the way education has influenced the people of different subgroups in the rural set up, any possible improvement qualitatively, the extent of utilisation of developmental programmes launched by state government and such other related aspects.

The Present Study

Education throughout the country is facing a crisis due to the lack of planning. This crisis can be overcome only through right education with proper emphasis on higher education. Higher Education is crucial for a country's development. The study covers all the factors responsible for the current status of Higher Education in the country. The present study will highlight the difficulties of the students coming for higher education. The students come forward, but their education gets stopped on the way the cause of which are under investigation of the study. As a result, the mechanism of higher education is hampered. Society suffers since it rears expenditure on them but receives very poor response. The economy starts reading down.

Objectives

This study of the district attempts: To examine the socio-economic background of the family of a student dropping out on the way, i.e., features in different classes to reach higher education

- To identify the cases whether rising out of first generation education.
- To analyse the problem arising out of ineffective teaching methods or due to the pattern of education prevalent at the elementary and secondary levels.
- To focus the study of different aspect like Administration, Organisation, Evaluation and Inspection, Teacher and Research practices etc., contributing to the piling up of the problem.
- To make circle-wise survey of all the school facilities presently made available in the district (The District-West Kameng has Eight Circles presently, i.e. Bhalukpong, Bomdila, Dirang, Jamiri, Kalaktang, Nafra, Singchung and Thrizino).
- To suggest in toto the measures to be taken for the expansion of higher education in the district.

Methodology

The project undertaken comprises an analytical survey of the existing school facilities, pre-service and in-service needs of the schools as well as college teachers (mention may be made that the said district has only one Degree college at its headquarters, Bomdila covering students from three districts, West Kameng, East Kameng and Tawang, established only a decade ago in 1988 and offering only Arts subjects that too Honours courses in three limited subjects, Economics, History and Political science). The study has been based basically on primary, secondary and tertiary sources, i.e., the officials records in the departmental files, committee reports, bound survey publication, inspection reports, published books, monograph and other printed materials at the state, district, circle, village and institutional levels.

Tools

For the collection of data for the study primarily the office of the DDSE (Deputy Director of School Education), West Kameng district, Bomdila, has been consulted. The said office has greatly come to the use for gathering information regarding the existing schools, infrastructure, enrolment, dropouts, teaching strength etc.

Moreover, three types of questionnaires were prepared and used for collecting data for analysing several factors contributing students dropping out. These are:

1) *Family Based Questionnaires (FBQ)* designed to collect informations regarding the family background of the student who has gone for drop out.
2) *Student Based Questionnaires (SBQ)* to elicit information on students' psychology, their opinion and difficulties behind the cause of dropping out.
3) *Teacher Based Questionnaires (TBQ)* to collect informations from the teachers appointed in the district in various capacities pertaining to the students problems, syllabus and other institutional facilities enjoyed by both the students and teachers.

The whole system has been empirically examined and analysed for a better solution.

Significance of the Study

Since education drives a nation's prosperity to a significant position, any kind of impediment to the progress of education is to be curbed out. Large number of academic drop outs not only hampers the study atmosphere in an institution but also drags the process of educational development of society in particular and of the country in general towards posterity. The study, the investigator hopes, would substantially lighten the burden of the explosive population growth of India.

A microscopic study of the problem and its suggestions for remedy after investigation if properly implemented would no doubt to some extent check the intensity of the problem. If this problem gets checked, the problem of unemployment gets lessened which enables a rural economy to grow stronger. If economy gets strengthened the sociological background of a society gets empowered. And a strong and powerful socio-economic background of a society accounts for the sum totality of nation's prosperity and development and projects India as one of leading nations in the world.

2

EDUCATION: THE PROPS FOR DEVELOPMENT

The world today has shrunk in size thanks to the advancement in communication. Some event which affects any one part of the globe immediately affects the other nations too. Distance is not barrier today. In adopting international understanding as a vital subject in education UNESCO has recommended in 1974 the guiding principles of education for international understanding. Promoting tolerance and friendship among all nations, racial or ethnic groups and furthering the activities of the UN towards the maintenance of peace, instilling positive attitudes towards peace, justice and human rights in young people are some of lendable principles underlying the concept of international understanding. Education for international understanding should start at an early age. The development of political knowledge, beliefs and values actually begins from infancy. Society today has become very complex. To understand and adjust to the complex concept of family, community, cultural groups, nation and the world pupils should be guided by teachers with the help of a spiral curriculum from the primary classes. At the secondary level students are able to learn and understand cognitively and effectively, the concepts and generalisations relating to international understanding and education for peace.

The curriculum at school needs to be modified to achieve the above mentioned goals. Cocurricular activities also offer wide scope for the practice of these ideas. The world today is interdependent and it is clear that different traditional programmes and the related disciplines are becoming internationalised. The trend towards infusing this state of mind in our educational system has become more progressive thanks to the world organs like the UNESCO. The modified perspective of education could be achieved through innovations in education for global interdependence and associated areas.

The Universal Declaration of Human Rights is another important charter that needs to be studied by students at the various levels. The articles enshrined in the Declaration could be taught to the students by internationalising it through a specific designed curriculum, so that the trainers will learn to transcend the narrow barriers of nationhood and step into the wider field of international understanding and peace.

Wherever we look, whether it be the developed countries or the newly developing countries, or even with our own country, those who are going ahead are those with education, with higher skills. Every country without exception which has developed economically in the past couple of centuries including all capitalist as well as socialist countries (like China) has made education (upto a minimum standard) of all citizens a primary responsibility of the state (Arun Ghosh: 85). One has to look at the history of Japan in the second half of the nineteenth century of China, South Korea, Taiwan, Thailand, Malaysia, Singapore, Hong Kong indeed all the success stories in the area of economic development in the second half of the twentieth century to realise that they all attached the highest importance to the education for all their citizens, commencing with primary education to all children as the first basic requirement of development of society.

One of the weakest parts of our constitution relates to the education in the fundamental rights of every citizen was limited, inter alia to the following : 'No citizen shall be denied admission into any educational institution maintained by the state or receiving aid out of state fund on grounds only of religion, race, caste, language or any of them. Again 'All minorities, whether based on religion or language, shall have the right to establish and administer educational institutions of their choice. These are essentially enabling rights, they do not ensure the right to education for every child, for every citizen, not do they ensure that the state must provide for the education of every child.

Even the Directive Principles of State Policy (in the constitution) merely suggest that the state shall within the limits of its economic capacity and development make effective provision for securing the right to work, to education and to public assistance in cases of unemployment, old age, sickness and disablement and in other cases of undeserved want.

While the planners, from early on, realised the importance of education as a means of improving the level of skills, of income and therefore, of the living standards of the people somewhere along the line the primary importance of education, not only as a means to an end but as an end in itself, was totally missed out.

Growth of Higher Education in India

Higher education in India in the modern sense of world, is less than one hundred and fifty years old. It is true, however, that in the long history of the country, beginning thousands of years before the Christian Era, centres of learning were existed in one form or another. Ancient Nalanda and Taxila universities have become synonymous with the highest achievements of education with certainty, for our information is based on documents of unequal date and unequal value. We only know that a definite conception of higher education did exist and that there were some centres of higher learning in ancient India (R.K. Mookherjee: 1938 and R.C. Majumdar: 1954).

However, upto the last decade of the eighteenth century, the British had not paid much attention to the instruction of western education in India schools and colleges (S. Nurullah and J.P. Naik: 1951; And University Education in India: 1956). Under the Macaulyian system of education (1835), education rapidly expanded, and English schools and colleges grew up in different parts of the country. The most important step towards the development of education was taken in 1854 (Woods Despatch) by which the three universities were founded on January 24, 1857 at Bombay, Calcutta and Madras.

The history of the first twenty five years of university education was mainly one of growth in the number of students and of colleges affiliated to the three existing universities. Private colleges were encouraged as a matter of policy because, they cost the state less than the government colleges and were considered more efficient. The increase in number of candidates for the examination and the vast extent of the area under the jurisdiction of the universities led to proposals for the establishment of new universities and new government colleges as well (University Education Commission: 1950 and Rajana Sidhanta: ch. 27). By 1946 the number of universities had grown to eighteen with about two thousand affiliated colleges attached to them. But there was no substantial change in the basic pattern of higher education which had somewhat crystallised by the beginning of the 20th century. Initially, the universities were not teaching bodies, they used to prescribe courses of study, conducted examinations and awarded diplomas to successful candidates. The actual teaching was one by colleges affiliated to the universities. These colleges were either government or private one, and were largely free to adopt their own ways of teaching and to appoint their own staff. The administration of the universities was vested in the Senate, consisting of a Chancellor (Governor of the state or Province), a Vice-Chancellor (the real head) and fellows who were nominated by the government and represented different branches of government. The senate was to delegate its executive authority in a Syndicate comprising the Vice-Chancellor and size fellows elected by the four faculties—Arts, Law, Medicine, and Engineering. The Syndicate was to appoint members of the various faculties. The Registrar was entrusted to manage the day to day administration of the universities. As a matter of fact, this pattern continues to govern most of the universities even today.

No doubt, the British Government from time to time appointed Commissions and committees to inquire into the objectives, problems and prospects of the universities in order to formulate some basic principles of educational policy. But the objectives were never clear excepting the two: to meet the urgent administrative needs of preparing natives for public appointment, and to promote English literature and science among the Indians. The increasing pressure of the students, changing politico-economic conditions during the last decade of the nineteenth century and early decades of the twentieth century compelled the government to readjust their administration and curriculum planning. The report of the Calcutta University Commission (1919) appointed in 1916 was a landmark in this respect which expressed some of the worst practices of private schools and colleges and made comprehensive recommendations dealing with, practically, every problem of secondary and University education. The 'Sergeant Report', prepared by the Government of India in 1944 viewed Indian education for the first time in the context of an awakened India during the British rule. But this plan was shelved and did not form the basis of national educational development when the independence came along (Post-war Educational Development: 1944 and J.P. Naik: 1955).

The Post-Independence Developments

In the Post-Independence era, realising the urgency and

importance of the role of the higher education, the Government of India appointed the University Education Commission (1948) under the chairmanship of S. Radhakrishnan to report on Indian university education and to suggest improvements and extensions to cope with the present and future requirements. The report of the Commission (1949) was the first comprehensive attempt at reorganisation of higher education since Independence.

In subsequent years the Government of India had accepted the recommendations of the Commission in principle, and several steps were taken to reorganise some aspects of the educational system, one such important was the establishment of the University Grants Commission in November 1953. The Commission was empowered to make grants to universities for new developments. In consequence, it has gradually assumed responsibilities for the promotion, development and coordination of university education on the one hand and to determine improve and maintain proper standards in teaching, examinations and research on the other. The Commission has over the years helped colleges and universities to upgrade their courses to the newly developed degree standards, to give their staff a higher scale of salaries to build libraries, laboratories, hostels and to institute a system of scholarship and fellowship for the students whose performance is considered superior.

In 1952, a Secondary Education Commission under the chairmanship of A.L. Mudaliar was appointed to survey, analyse and provide guidelines for the problems of secondary education. It presented its report in 1953. After the report was submitted, a good deal of follow-up action was taken like the conversion of high schools into higher secondary schools, development of multipurpose schools with provision for a number of elective subjects, expansion and improvement of facilities for the teaching of science, provision of educational and vocational guidance, improvement of the examination and evaluation system, enlargement of facilities for vocational education, increased facilities for the education of girls and the backward classes and encouragement to merit scholarship (Third Five Year Plan: 584). In the educational history of the country, the secondary stage of education was correctly defined in the Report of the Secondary Education commission, for the first time, as a self-sufficient course preparing students to enter life after completing the course (Hans Nagpaul: 202). Moreover, on All-India Council for Secondary Education (AICSE) was set up in 1955. It functioned for a few years. The four regional colleges of Education eventually taken over by the NCERT, were established during this period in Ajmer, Bhopal, Bhubaneswar and Mysore (*EPW:* vol. XXXII: 881).

The NCERT, established in the early 1960s, became an umbrella organisation for the entire grant of education before the university stage and secondary education also came under its purview. Without going into details of what the NCERT has been able to accomplishing respect of secondary education, one valuable initiative taken by it deserves to be acknowledged as having been put through with a certain degree of thoroughness. This refers to the remodelling of question papers set in different examinations. The intention was both to influence teaching and testing. In view of repeated critical observations of committee and commissions about the subordination of the teaching system to the examination system, it was felt that immediate attention had to be given to the conduct of examinations. This initiative bore some fruit as described also.

The Kothari Commission which was appointed in 1964 and which reported in 1966, had given considerable attention to school education. It recommended Indian education needs a drastic reconstruction, almost a revolution. We need to bring about major improvements in the effectiveness of primary education, to introduce work-experience as an integral part of general education; to vocationalise secondary education; to improve the quality of teachers in sufficient strength to liquidate illiteracy to strengthen centres of advanced studies and strive to attain in some of our universities at least, higher international standards; to lay special emphasis in the combination of teaching and research; to pay particular attention to education and research in agriculture and allied sciences. All this calls for a determined and large-scale action. Tinkering with the existing situation, and moving forward with faltering steps and lack of faith can make things worse than before (Education Commission, 1966: 01).

Its recommendations however, did not get implemented to the extent that they should have. But that is for reasons which do not have to be considered here. Two of these reasons, however, may be identified, for they have continued to influence the carrier and growth of the secondary system. One was the extraordinary growth of population in the first quarter century after Independence. The crucial decade in this respect was the decade of 1950s. The death rate came down by about 10 per cent during that decade with the result that the population began to boom and has not since stopped increasing. Coupled with it was a marked deterioration in the temper and tone of political decision-making. The three-year holiday from planning during 1966-69 was an expression of these unhappy conditions on the economic front. Though the initiative was somewhat recovered with the launching of the Fourth Plan, the two factors described above continued to operate in a manner and this affected secondary education in a manner which brought out its deficiencies and infirmities further (EPW: XXII: 881).

After India became free, the first National Policy of Education was issued in 1968 to promote national progress, effective citizenship and culture and to achieve national integration. This policy stressed the need for a radical reconstruction of the educational system with the aim of improving quality. On the one hand, it recommended the development of science and technology, on the other, emphasis was laid on the cultivation of values and a closer relationship between education and the life of the people. In toto, the National policy stressed (i) free and compulsory education upto the age of 14; (ii) improved status and emoluments of teachers; (iii) adoption of the three-language formula and development of regional languages; (iv) equalisation of education service and research; (v) development of education for agriculture and industry; (vi) improvement on quality and production of inexpensive text-books and (vii) investment of 6 percent of national income on education (B.L. Grover: 355). The new pattern of education proposed was the 10+2+3 pattern for the whole of India. Now in ninety per cent of our villages we have schools within a radius of one kilometer. The 10+2+3 pattern has been accepted in all parts of the country. The first ten years are split into 5+3+2 years of primary, upper primary and secondary schools respectively.

By the Constitutional Amendment of 1976, education was placed on the Concurrent List which meant greater responsibility for both the centre and the states. The states responsibility remained the same as before. But the centre was to take up more responsibility for developing education to integrate the whole nation. The objectives included, maintenance of quality and standards of education (including those of the teaching profession at all levels), manpower development, research and international understanding all to promote excellence at all levels of the educational pyramid throughout the country (S. Lakshmi: 115).

The same policy was reiterated in the National Policy on Education of 1986 which talked of a National System of Education. This system implied that upto a given level, all students, irrespective of caste, creed, location or sex should be provided with education of a comparable quality. It envisaged a common core curriculum with a provision to include the history of India's freedom movement, the constitutional obligations and other contents essential to nurture national identity promoting cultural and social values, democracy, egalitarianism, equality of the sexes, secularism, environmental protection, removal of social barriers observance of the small family norm and development of scientific attitude.

The new policy laid special emphasis on the removal of disparities and to equalise educational opportunity by attending to the specific needs of those who have been denied equality so far (empowerment of women, equalisation of opportunity for SC/ST, for minorities, the handicapped) particularly rural people and tribals were given the maximum encouragement. It was realised that the formal education alone would not able to launch this daunting task. Hence a vast programme of adult and containing education was implemented through various ways and channels, including establishment of rural centres for continuing education; workers education through the employers, use of radio, TV and films as mass and group learning media; creation of learners groups and organisations; programme of distance education; organising assistance in self-learning; organising need and interest-based vocational training programmes (Inderpal Singh: 82).

Reorganising the holistic nature of child development early childhood care and education (ECCE) was given high priority. ECCE programmes were made child oriented and focused around play and individual differences. Child-centered-activity based education was recommended. The first generation learners are allowed to learn at their own pace. Whenever required they are to be provided with remedial programmes and other instructional strategies. The primary schools are being provided with all infrastructural facilities such as school buildings with adequate class rooms equipment and teaching aids for learning. Provision was made that in the remote areas where the school today has one teacher, two teachers will be provided of whom one will be a woman.

A phased drive, termed Operation Blackboard was undertaken to improve primary schools all over the country. Construction of school buildings was given the first priority from the NREP and RLEGP funds.

Non-formal education (NFE) was launched for school dropouts, for children from areas without schools working children and girls which could not attend regular day schools. The NFE centres were given adequate teaching aids for the provision of a proper learning environment. Dedicated men and women from the locality were selected to serve as instructors who were given special training for the purpose. Steps were too taken to facilitate non-formal students, entry into the formal system.

The problem of dropouts at the primary level has been tried to be tackled for which meticulously formulated strategies are being adopted based on micro planning percolating down to the grass roots level all over the country to ensure retention of children at school. All children who attained the age of 11 years by 1990, did five years of schooling or its equivalent through non-formal education. Similarly by 1995, all children upto 14 years of age were provided free and compulsory education.

A new experiment in education was initiated by establishing new kind of schools with new orientation called **Navodaya Vidayalayas** which provide accelerated and good quality of education to all talented children hailed from the rural parts, irrespective of their capacity to pay for education. The broad aim of this project is to bring out the talents and aptitudes in children and direct towards excellence. The scheme has one of its objectives, the achievement of national integration in children drawn from various parts of India.

Improvement of vocational education is another laudable goal of the new education policy. This takes into consideration the preparation of students for identified occupations which would include several areas of activity. Vocational courses are offered after the secondary stage and in special cases after class eighth. The major objectives behind the vocational education are to develop the attitudes, knowledge and skills required for entrepreneurship and self-employment. Graduates of such courses are given opportunities for professional growth, carrier improvement and later entry into courses of general, technical and professional education through appropriate bridge courses. The main target was to provide vocational education to 10 per cent of higher secondary students by 1990 and 25 per cent by 1995.

A beginning was made in de-linking degree from jobs in selected areas. The proposal could not be applied to occupation specific course like engineering, medicine, law, teaching, etc. Delinking was applied in services where a university degree was not a necessary qualification. Concomitant with delinking, an appropriate machinery such as a National Testing Service was to be established, to conduct tests on a voluntary basis to determine suitability of candidates for specified jobs and to pave the way for the emergence of norms of comparable competence across the nation.

As part of sound educational strategy examinations are to be reoriented in order to bring about qualitative improvements in education. The objective was to recast the examination system so as to ensure a method of assessment to measure students development. In functional terms this meant elimination of excessive element of chance and subjectivity, deemphasis of memorisation, continuous and comprehensive evaluation of both the scholastic and non-scholastic aspects of education; introduction of concomitant changes in instructional materials and methodology introduction of the semester system from the secondary stage in a phased manner, the use of grades in place of marks.

It is said that no people can rise above the level of its teachers. The Government and the community should endeavour to create condition which will help motivate and inspire teachers on constructive and creative lines. Teachers should have the freedom to innovate, to devise appropriate methods of communication and activities relevant to the needs and capabilities of and the concerns of the community. Educational technology was employed in the spread of useful information, the training and retraining of teachers to improve quality, sharpen awareness of art and culture, inculcate abiding values etc., both in the formal and non-formal sectors.

The National Policy also recommended the reorganisation of technical and management education. In this context, the education department (also the department of human resources development) at the centre encouraged computer education at all levels right from the +2 stage. The All India Council for Technical Education was provided with the authority for planning, formulation and maintenance of norms and standards, accredition, funding of priority areas, monitoring and evaluation maintaining parity of certification and awards and coordinating and integrating development of technical and management education.

The policy suggested the revamping of higher education. Based on the feedback regarding colleges affiliated to universities autonomous colleges were to develop in large numbers. Similarly, autonomy was encouraged for departments in the universities. State level planning and coordination of higher education was attempted through councils of higher education. UGC was to encourage research by providing financial help and ensuring high quality in the universities and in the affiliated colleges. Research in indology, humanities and social sciences was to be encouraged. Open universities were to be encouraged to provide higher education as an instrument of democratisation of education.

Education Outlay in Five Year Plans

Provision of educational opportunities to the people has been an important programme in the education sector since the planning era. Educational outlay in the various five years plans has been shown in Table 2.1.

Table 2.1: Educational Outlay in the Various Five Year Plans

(Rs. in crores)

Five Year Plan	*Total Plan Outlay*	*Expenditure on Education*	*Percentage of Total Plan Outlay*
1	2	3	4
First Plan (1951-56)	1960	153	7.8
Second Plan (1956-61)	4672	273	5.8
Third Plan (1961-66)	8577	589	6.8
Annual Plans (1966-69)	6625	323	4.8
Fourth Plan (1969-74)	15,779	786	4.9
Fifth Plan (1974-79)	39,426	1285	3.2
Sixth Plan (1980-85)	97,500	2530	2.5
Seventh Plan (1985-90)	1,80,000	7633	4.2
Eighth Plan (1992-97)	4,35,000	19,600	4.5
Ninth Plan (1997-02)	NA	NA	NA

Source: Compiled from various Five Year Plans.

The table reveals that expenditure on education has been rising in each Five Year Plan, but the expenditure on education as percentage of total plan outlay has been fluctuating (dominating decreasing) during the successive Five Years Plans. The relative importance given to education has been declining gradually over the years from 7.8 percent in the First Five Year plan to 2.5 percent in the Sixth. Thanks to the National Policy on Education (1986) it is only during the Seventh and Eighth Five Year Plans, this declining trend was reversed. The Eighth Plan allocation was quite high, 4.5 percent; but it is still much less than the proportion allocated in the First Plan.

It appears thus there are three important phases in the allocation of resources to education in the Five Year Plans. During the first three Five-Year Plan periods, the allocation to education had been more than 5 per cent. Even though it declined in the second plan, the decline was immediately checked in the third plan. The second phase consisting of the fourth, fifth and sixth plans was characterized by a consistent decline in the plan allocation to education. The seventh and eight five years plans formed the third phase when efforts were made to check the declining trend and to substantially increase the allocation to education. One can only hope that the efforts will continue during the Ninth Five Year Plan and beyond.

Expenditure on elementary education, secondary education, university education during various plans has been shown in Table 2.2.

Two trends are obvious from the figures shown in Table 2.2. One is the sharp decline in the outlay on elementary education during the first three plans and the steep increase in the same period. The second is the outlay on secondary education which was maintained at a more or less steady rate except for the first plan period. To what extent the two phenomena are inter-related is a matter that need not be discussed here.

This much should be clear, however, that there is a certain degree of interrelationship among the allocations to various sectors of education. Depending upon the resources available the outlay on education has been rising

Table 2.2: Plan Expenditure on Different Sectors of Education

Sector	*1st Plan*	*2nd Plan*	*3rd Plan*	*Annual Plans*	*4th Plan*	*5th Plan*	*6th Plan*	*7th Plan*	*1990-92*	*8th Plan*
1	2	3	4	5	6	7	8	9	10	11
Elementary	(85) 56	(95) 35	(201) 34	(75) 25	(239) 30	(410) 32	(836) 33	(2849) 37	(1729) 37	(9201) 47
Secondary	(20) 13	(51) 19	(103) 18	(53) 16	(140) 18	(250) 19	(530) 21	(1832) 24	(1053) 22	(3498) 18
Adult	–	–	–	–	–	–	(224) 9	(470) 6	(416) 9	(1848) 9
Higher	(14) 9	(48) 18	(87) 15	(77) 24	(195) 25	(292) 23	(559) 22	(1201) 16	(588) 12	(1516) 8
Others	(14) 9	(30) 10	(73) 12	(37) 11	(106) 14	(177) 14	(108) 4	(198) 3	(118) 2	(751) 4
Techical	(20) 13	(49) 18	(125) 21	(181) 25	(106) 13	(156) 12	(273) 11	(1083) 14	(823) 17	(2786) 14
Total	**(153) 100**	**(273) 100**	**(589) 100**	**(323) 100**	**(786) 100**	**(1285) 100**	**(2530) 100**	**(7633) 100**	**(4727) 100**	**(19600) 100**

Notes: (i) Figures in parentheses in crores of rupees.
(ii) Figures shown below parentheses in percentage.

Source: 'Education for All', Department of Education, Ministry of Human Resource Development.

or falling. As stated earlier two sectors of education (elementary education and higher and professional education) were given increased importance in the height of the social pressures that were bring exerted. Therefore, the order of priority kept fluctuating. On the other hand, secondary education was never locked upon as an independent of self-contained sector of education. Expenditure on secondary education had to be incurred largely because there was pressure from below (*EPW:* XXXII: 881).

Against the backdrop of the growth and development of education in India after independence resources allocated on education in various Five year plans, resources allocated on various sectors of education and analysis discussed above it will be more useful if we bring about a review of the progress of the five decade-old life of education so as to understand the achievements and failures. Let us have a look at the changing scenario of the educational system in India. Table 2.3 gives an overall picture of the growth of recognised educational institutions since 1951.

The Table shows that within a period of four decades, between 1950-51 to 1991-92, while the number of primary schools increased by a quotient of 2.7, that of Middle, Secondary and Higher Secondary increased almost by parallel quotient, i.e. 11.2 and 11.1 respectively. The number of institutions meant for higher education also grew significantly, by a quotient of 9.1.

Elementary Education

The data reflecting the progress of elementary education in India have been presented in the Table 2.4.

As a consequence of the vast expansion of primary education, Indian elementary education system has become one of the largest educational systems of the world. The system providing accessibility within one kilometer of walking distance to 8.25 lakh habitations, covering 94 per

Table 2.3: Growth of Recognised Educational Institutions Since 1951

Institutions	*1950-51*	*1960-61*	*1970-71*	*1980-81*	*1991-92*	*Increase in between 1950-51 and 1991-92 by quotient*	
1. Primary	209671	330399	408378	455538	565786	2.7	
2. Middle	13596	49663	90621	116447	152077	11.2	
3. Secondary/ Higher Secondary	7288	17257	36738	51594	81201	11.1	
4. Colleges for General Education	498	1043	2598	3425	5058	10.27	−9.1
5. Colleges for Professional Education*	155	696	2398	724**	950**	NA	
6. Universities	27	45	82	110	196@	7.2	

Notes: * Includes engineering, technology, architecture, medicine, agriculture and forestry, veterinary science and teacher training institutes upto 1970-71.

** Includes only engineering, technology, medicine and teacher training colleges.

@ Includes Deemed to be universities and Institutes of National Importance.

Source: Compiled from Ministry of Education; *Education for All of 2000*, 1990 and *Selected Educational Statistics*, 1991-92.

Table 2.4: Progress of Education in India (Elementary)

		1950-51	1993-94
No. of Institutions (in lakhs)			
Primary Schools (I-V)		2.10	5.73
Upper Primary Schools (VI-VIII)		0.13	1.55
	Total	**2.23**	**7.28**
No. of Teachers (lakhs)			
Primary Schools		5.38	17.03
Upper Primary Schools		0.36	10.80
	Total	**5.74**	**27.83**
Gross Enrolment			
Primary Stage			
Total Enrolment (lakhs)		192.00	1,082.00
Gross Enrolment Ratio (%)		43.10	104.50
Upper Primary Stage			
Total Enrolment (lakhs)		31.00	399.00
Gross Enrolment (%)		12.00	67.70

Source: Journal of Educational Planning and Administration, Volume X, No. 3, July 1996.

cent of the total population of India while 85.4 per cent of the population is served with a middle school within a distance of three kilometers. Despite the fact that gross enrolment ratio (i.e. enrolment as a proportion of the population in the relevant age group, 6-11) for primary level reached 104.5 per cent the literacy rate was still merely 52.2 per cent as per the 1991 census.

Let us take a quick look at the emerging pattern. Table 2.4 gives a brief summary picture of the growth of recognised elementary educational institutions since 1951. Between 1950-51 and 1993-94 the number of elementary schools (both primary and upper primary) increased by a quotient of 3.2 and that of the teachers by a quotient of 4.8. The proportion of teachers in relation to primary schools is brought out in Table 2.5 (data taken upto 1987-88) which would further illustrate the general neglect of primary education. It would be seen that nearly three out of the primary schools had one teacher (or none) and more than six out of ten had upto ten teachers only (Arun Ghosh: 95). Moreover, the fifth All India Educational Survey conducted in 1986 found that 28 per cent of primary schools in the country have single-teacher schools and another 32 per cent had two teachers each (NCERT: 1992).

Table 2.5: Primary Schools According to Teachers in Position, 1987-88

No. of Teachers in Position	*No. of Schools*	*Percentage of Total Schools*
0	2628	0.50
1	148033	27.96
2	171389	32.38
3	80365	15.00
4	47188	8.19
5 and above	79789	15.07
Total	**529392**	**100.00**

Source: Arun Ghosh: 1995.

Secondary Education

In a developed country, literacy is almost universal and children stay at school till the ages of 16,17,18 as the case may be and drop out after completing their secondary education. In most cases secondary education is the terminal stage of education. Till some decades ago only a small percentage even less than 10 per cent of the relevant student population, elected to go to the college. Of late however, the situation has been changing. Underdeveloped countries are in a different position. Most of them face a difficult situation in several aspects, particularly in the field of social services. The resources available for education are generally meagre though the percentage varies from country to country. Currently India spends around 3.5 per cent of its national income on education. It is proposed to raise this percentage to 6 by the end of the Ninth Plan.

Generally speaking secondary education in India has got a very poor deal. In terms of argument in hand, it will however be in order to mention two factors. One was the decision of the Constitution makers to make education compulsory upto the age of 14. That the decision has not been properly implemented is another issue. The commitment is there and has become a point of reference for all subsequent discussions on the problem. The second was the preeminence which higher education has enjoyed ever since the establishment of the universities in India in 1857. The fruits of that preeminence were properly reflected on the architecture of Indian Constitution and not withstanding their background and training almost each of the principal architects of the constitution recognised the importance of universal education. That is how Article 45 of the Constitution came into existence.

Secondary education was nowhere in the picture in this landscape of the future India. Further, those at the helm of affairs did not recommend compulsory education beyond the age of 14. This was not regarded as feasible or advisable at that stage of the country's development. The elementary education was perceived as an essential objective and everything else including secondary education was perceived as desirable. In consequence secondary education did not receive the requisite attention. This had unhappy consequences for the future of secondary education and it will be difficult to say whether those adverse consequences have been taken care of adequately and properly even till today. And if India has to progress in a meaningful sense secondary education will have to be given its due. This situation has not remained frozen at the point when India became independent half a century ago. It has been evolving and will continue to do so.

According to the provisional statistics released by the NCERT in respect of the Sixth All India Educational Survey the growth of schools from 1986 to 1993 was as follows (*EPW:* XXXII: 880).

Table 2.6: Increase in Type of Schools

Types of Schools	*Percentage Increase*
Primary	8.78
Upper Primary	15.75
Secondary	25.84
Higher Secondary	52.11

It is clear that both secondary and higher secondary levels of education are growing at an unusually fast pace. The relatively massive growth of education at the lower levels during the preceding decades had made it more or less inevitable. In contrast the figures given in Table 2.6 suggest that primary education has not been growing at an equally fast rate. Presumably the base in respect of primary education has become somewhat large and therefore the rate of growth, when seen in terms of percentage does not appear to be all that notable. Whatever be the explanation the fact remains that there has been a spurt in the growth of secondary and higher secondary schools during recent years. In terms of the percentage increase of teachers another item of data conforms the above calculation. The exact figures are as follows.

Table 2.7: Increase in Teachers by Types of Schools

Types of Schools	*Percentage Increase*
Primary	11.27
Upper Primary	10.35
Secondary	15.92
Higher Secondary	40.12

One more relevant piece of evidence may be seen from the details of the newly established schools during this period in respect of that much neglected area of social analysis the rural-urban divide:

Table 2.8: Increase in Secondary and Higher Secondary Schools in Rural and Urban Areas

Types of Schools	*Percentage Increase*
(i) Secondary	
Rural	24.19
Urban	30.51
Total	**25.84**
(ii) Higher Secondary	
Rural	63.14
Urban	42.66
Total	**52.11**

The figures given in Tables 2.6 to 2.8 point to the new developments that are taking place. Increasing number of students are electing to for higher secondary education (52.11 per cent). In the existing circumstances this means that more students will in course of time, opt for entry into colleges. Hence it is necessary to recognise the importance of secondary education, re-examine the curriculum of the relevant classes and streamline the working of School Education Board.

Higher Education

Ever since education came to be imparted in a well organised fashion, schools and colleges were established in India both under public (government) and private auspices. While universities were set up exclusively under the state auspices, colleges and schools were founded by both state and private agencies. Ever since the establishment of the universities in India in 1857 higher education enjoyed a status quo of its own. It was the gateway to a prosperous career and all those who managed to cross the earlier hurdles were keen to opt for higher education. Presently India is not in a position to align the rate of growth on the field of education with the rate of growth of the economy. The only way to deal with the problem is to improve diversity and streamline secondary education make it terminal in character so that the pressure at the level of higher education is relieved.

But today's education system is producing an increasing number of 'unemployables' and the problem of the educated unemployed (in the urban areas particularly) is beginning to create social tensions which can no longer be ignored. The constitutional directive of providing free universal elementary education remains as the most conspicuous failure of India during 50 years of Independence and no signs of its fulfillment could be noted until the early next century at the earliest. Rural urban inequalities, gender differences, differences by castes all have decreased, but they are still sizeable. Enrolment ratio in higher education is a meagre 5 per cent of the eligible age group population, while an enrolment ratio of 29 per cent in higher education seems to be a threshold level for an economy to become an economically advanced country.

In recent days the changes in policies and approaches towards financing education particularly higher education are noteworthy. Most of the recent policy debates have been around the question: who should pay for higher education? This is in contrast to the past when questions relating to financing of higher education revolved around improving the mechanism of allocation of public resources to it. The economic reforms have added new colour to this question. With an increasing strong opinion that welfare state is dead, the conventionally strong role of the state is financing education as a whole is under attack. 'Public good', the nature of education is no more recognised as an important aspect; education, higher education in particular is regarded as a 'non-merit' good public subsidies on which could be drastically reduced, if not eliminated altogether. 'Privatisation' of education is no more considered undesirable; in fact, it is argued to be offering an effective solution to major educational problems.

Privatisation which was not a respectable term in 1950s and later, has become a fashionable slogan in 1990s. Policy debates on improved allocation of resources are being replaced by discussion on how to adopt various strategies of cost recovery (*EPW:* XXXII, No. 36: 2240). Methods of cost recovery have elaborately been discussed (E.T. Mathew: *EPW,* 1996: 867-68). Measures such as fees which have been either symbolic or served only a marginal role in financing education are being viewed as the most important potential source of funds for education. It should be realised that in few developed countries this has been the case. For instance, about 15 per cent of the recurrent costs of higher education in India are recovered from the students in the form of fees; the corresponding proportion is the same in public universities in the US and much less in many European universities.

Discussions on fee reforms that used to be confined to higher education have started sneaking into secondary and primary education as well. Considerations for equality in education are giving place to considerations of efficiency.

The poor do not prominently figure any more in discussions on financing education as if education is 'luxury good' meant for the rich only and that of higher education for the richer.

It is important to note that efforts are under way in many states in India to streamline the fee system in colleges and universities. Full cost recovery however, is ruled out; just as heavy subsidisation of higher education is theoretically unsound, full-cost recovery of costs of higher education from the consumers is not favoured since all education, whatever be the level generates external benefits of varying degrees. Instead, the aim should be partial but substantial cost recovery in higher education.

Agreed that there is a genuine case for raising fees in universities and colleges, what should be the extent of the upward division? This is indeed a theory problem. In general we may caution that the upward revision should not be such that vast sections of students are forced to opt out of higher education. In economies like India which are characterised by high rates of unemployment there is also the additional danger that very high fees at the university/ college level might reduce demand for secondary education as secondary education does not provide adequate employment opportunities. In order to reduce the adverse impact of a sudden hike in fees, it may be desirable to carry out the revision in a phased manner.

Moreover, any enhancement of tuition fee would surely make it impossible for some sections to go in for higher education. To enable such sections to get enrolled in institutions of higher education a liberal system of student loans is often recommended. It is argued that the poor but well-motivated students could avail the loans, enrol themselves the institutions of higher learning, get employed on successful completion of their respective course and repay the loans as and when they are able to do so. Student loans are strongly recommended in terms of both equity and efficiency (Blaug: 1970). In the Indian context student loans have an added disadvantage. When higher education does not generate employment and as repayment of loans becomes compulsory, young graduates of poor households will be the worst affected. This limitation however does not apply to all forms of higher education; professional graduates are not in the same predicament as ordinary graduates; the lot of commerce and business administration graduates is generally much better than that of arts and science graduates.

In toto, Higher education offers ample opportunities for participation by both private and public sectors. The inadequacies or rigidities arising from exclusive reliance on either sector or any one form of private initiative can and should be corrected by diversifying the mode of financing. Whether individual institutions of higher education are formally classified as public/private or not the most sensible option under the privilege conditions in India is not only to broaden the financial base of higher education but also to restructure higher education in terms of courses and content in order to make it relevant (without, of course, neglecting basic sciences and research).

Growth of Literacy and Gender Inequalities

Data about growth of literacy have been provided for 1951 to 1991 in Table 2.9. It may be noted that literacy rates for 1951, 1961 and 1971 relate to population aged 5 years and above. For 1981 and 1991 however the data relate to population aged 7 years and above. Although these two sets of figures are not strictly comparable, still they can be used to indicate a broad trend.

The data reveal that literacy rate improved from 18.3 per cent in 1951 to 34.5 per cent in 1971 and rose further to 52.2 per cent in 1991. But the literacy rate of males which

Table 2.9: Literacy Rates in India: 1951-1991

Year	*Persons*	*Males*	*Females*	*Male/Female Disparity Rate*
1951	18.33	27.16	8.86	3.1
1961	28.31	40.40	15.34	2.6
1971	34.45	45.95	21.97	2.1
1981	43.67	56.50	29.85	1.9
1991	52.21	64.13	39.29	1.6

Note: The 1981 figures do not include data for Assam and the 1991 figures for Jammu & Kashmir since the respective census could not be held there.

Source: Compiled and computed from *Census of India 1991,* series 1, paper 1 of 1991.

was 27.2 per cent in 1951 rose to about 46 per cent in 1971 and then increased further to 64.1 per cent in 1991. There is no doubt that there has been an appreciable growth in female literacy from 8.9 per cent in 1951 to about 22 per cent in 1971 and further to 39.3 per cent in 1991.

Disparity ratio between male and female literacy which was 3.1 in 1951 declined to 2.1 in 1971 and further in 1991. This is due to the fact female literacy during the last 40 years has been growing at a faster rate than male literacy. This has certainly narrowed the disparity ratio between male-female literacy. During the last 40 years, female literacy has increased by 343 per cent and male literacy grew by 136 per cent. This is a healthy trend and needs to be strengthened.

Another method of analysing the male-female literacy ratio is to examine the male and female literacy rate in rural and urban areas. Table 2.10 provides a back-up of male and female literacy rate for 1981 and 1991.

Table 2.10: Disparity Ratio Male and Female Literacy

	Literacy between Rural and Urban Areas		
	Male (1)	*Female* (2)	*Disparity Ratio* (3)=(1)/(2)
Rural Areas			
1981	49.7	21.8	2.28
1991	57.8	30.3	1.91
Urban Areas			
1981	76.8	56.4	1.36
1991	81.0	63.9	1.27

Source: Journal of Education Planning and Administration, Vol. X, No. 3, July' 1996: 258.

The data reveal that male literacy rate improved from 49.7 per cent to 57.8 per cent in rural areas during 1981 and 1991, whereas female literacy rate increased from 21.8 per cent to 30.3 per cent. The disparity ratio declined from 2.28 to 1.91. As against this, the situation in urban areas was much better. Male literacy improved from 76.8 per cent in 1981 to 81.0 per cent in 1991, whereas female literacy improved from 56.4 per cent to 63.9 per cent during the decade. Consequently, the disparity ratio declined from 1.36 to 1.27. This only signifies the fact that urbanisation has a great positive effect on improving female literacy.

Literacy: Regional Scenario

There is a very wide variation experience in the different states of India. Kerala stands at the top achieving an overall literacy rate of about 90 per cent as against the national average of 5.22 per cent in overall literacy, 64 per cent in male literacy and 39.3 per cent in female literacy. Mizoram, Goa, Maharashtra, Himachal Pradesh, Tamil Nadu, Nagaland, Gujarat, Tripura have achieved overall literacy rates of over 70 per cent and above and thus could be described as **'high'** literacy rates. But paradoxically some of these high literacy states have not achieved even 50 per cent level in female literacy. However, Gujarat, Tripura and Manipur have lagged behind in female literacy.

'Medium' literacy states are those which have an overall literacy between 50 and 60 per cent, male literacy between 60 and 70 per cent and female literacy between 40 and 50 per cent. Manipur, Punjab, West Bengal, Sikkim, Karnatak, Haryana and Assam are among the medium literacy states.

'Low' literacy states are those which have an overall literacy rate of less than 50 per cent male literacy rate between 50 and 60 per cent and female literacy rate between 20 to 40 per cent. Among the poor performs on the literacy front are Meghalaya, Orissa, Madhya Pradesh, Andhra Pradesh, Uttar Pradesh, Rajasthan and Bihar. Arunachal Pradesh too falls in this category presenting an overall literacy rate of 41.59 per cent, male literacy rate of 51.45 per cent and female literacy rate of 29.69 per cent.

The male-female literacy disparity ratios indicate that Kerala and Mizoram have achieved a near ideal situation with this ratio touching 1.1 level. States and UTs with a **low** disparity ratio below 1.25 are Kerala, Mizoram, Lakshadweep, Chandigarh, Goa, Delhi and Nagaland. States with **medium** disparity ratio between 1.25 and 1.50 are Maharashtra, Himachal Pradesh, Tamil Nadu, Nagaland, Gujarat, Tripura, Manipur, Punjab, West Bengal, Assam, Meghalaya and Pondicherry. States with **high** disparity ratio, i.e. more than 1.5 are Sikkim, Harayana, Orissa, Andhra Pradesh, Madhya Pradesh, Uttar Pradesh, Arunachal Pradesh, Rajasthan and Bihar. Orissa, Andhra Pradesh, Madhya Pradesh, Uttar Pradesh, Rajasthan and Bihar are the six states which account for 202.6 million literacy. These six states account for 63.2 per cent of the total illiterates, out of which male illiterate are 64.5 per cent and female illiterates 62.3 per cent (Rudar Datt: JEPA: 260).

Literacy Rates of Scheduled Castes and Scheduled Tribes

We have the data about the literacy ratio among Scheduled Castes (SCs) and Scheduled Tribes (STs) alongwith overall literacy rate. As against an overall literacy rate of 52.2 per cent, literacy rate among SCs was 37.4 per cent and that among STs was 29.6 per cent. There is a high degree of variation among states regarding SC literacy rate as high as about 80 per cent in Kerala, Mizoram, Goa, Maharashtra, Himachal Pradesh, Gujarat, Tripura, Manipur, Sikkim, Assam and Arunachal Pradesh. States below the national average of 37.4 per cent are Orissa, Madhya Pradesh, Andhra Pradesh, Uttar Pradesh, Rajasthan and Bihar. Mention may be made here that Arunachal Pradesh does not have SCs as its original inhabitants and census on its SCs includes SCs on service sector (0.47%).

The literacy rate of STs also varies between 17.2 per cent in case of Andhra Pradesh to about 83 per cent in the case of Mizoram. Kerala shows ST literacy rate of 57.2 per cent, but this seems to be due to very small proportion of ST population (1.1%) in the total population. Lakshadweep and Mizoram with bulk of their population being that of STs (93-94%) are devoting all their efforts to improve their literacy rates. Orissa and Madhya Pradesh which have large ST population have not paid adequate attention to improve literacy among STs.

SC/ST Enrolment at Various Stages of Education

Basing upon the Annual Report (1994-95) of the Ministry of Human Resource Development Table 2.11 has been prepared which provides data about total enrolment and the share of SCs and the STs at various stages.

Table 2.11: Proportion of SCs and STs in Total Enrolment as on September 30, 1993

Level	*SC Enrolment*	*ST Enrolment*	*Non SC/ST Enrolment*	*Total Enrolment*
Primary	75.8 (16.2)	85.9 (7.9)	820.3 (75.8)	1082.01 (100.0)
Middle	55.8 (14.0)	21.9 (5.5)	321.4 (80.5)	399.1 (100.00)
Secondary/ Higher Secondary	28.1 (12.0)	9.9 (4.2)	195.4 (83.7)	233.4 (100.0)
Higher Education	3.9 (8.5)	1.3 (2.8)	40.5 (88.6)	45.7 (100.0)

Notes: Figures in parentheses are percentages of total enrolment in the row.

This table denotes that at the primary level, share of SCs in total enrolment of 1,082 lakhs in 1993-94 was 16.2 per cent and that of STs was 7.9 per cent. This is broadly in consonance with the share of SCs in total population (16.7 per cent) and that of STs in total population (7.9 per cent). But as we move higher into the structure the share of SCs and STs indicates a continuous decline. At the middle level, SCs share falls to 14.0 per cent, at secondary/higher secondary level it declines further to 12 per cent and still further gets reduced to 8.5 per cent as against 7.9 per cent at the primary level, at the secondary/higher secondary level it falls further to 4.2 per cent and gets squeezed to just 2.8 per cent at the higher education level. Consequently as we move higher in the educational structure, the share of non SC/ST enrolment shows an increasing trend.

Tables 2.12 and Table 2.13 (Department of Education, Annual Report 1994-95) provide information about enrolment at various stages-sex wise. The data represent that as we move higher in the structure, the disparity ratio between the enrolment of boys and girls shows an increase from 1.33 at the primary level to 1.54 at the middle level, 1.89 at the secondary/higher secondary level and 1.98 at higher education level. The situation is within the case of SCs but relatively less in intensity among the STs. The disparity ratio at the higher education level among SCs was 2.89, whereas it was 2.25 in case of STs. Similarly disparity ratio at secondary/higher secondary level for SCs was 2.39 and that of STs was 2.19. Since STs are concentrated in a few states and form a considerable part of the total population of these states, as in the case of Arunachal Pradesh, Lakshadweep, Manipur, Meghalaya, Mizoram and Nagaland, greater effort is made as consequence of the tribal psychology of group behaviours accepting the directions of the tribal chief and subsequently a greater dent has been made in providing educational facilities to the tribal population.

Table 2.12: Enrolment by Stages in India as on September 30, 1993

(in lakhs)

Level	*Boys*	*Girls*	*Total*	*Disparity Ratio*
Primary	618.0 (57.1)	464.0 (42.0)	1082.0 (100.0)	1.33
Middle	242.1 (60.7)	157.0 (39.3)	399.1 (100.0)	1.54
Secondary/ Higher Secondary	152.7 (65.4)	80.7 (34.6)	233.4 (100.0)	1.89
Higher Education	30.4 (66.5)	15.3 (33.5)	45.7 (100.0)	1.98

Dropout Rates Major Factor for Low Level Literacy

Table 2.14 provides the trends of dropout rates in India from the primary to the secondary level for the years 1980-81 to 1993-94.

Table 2.13: Enrolment of SCs and STs as on September 30, 1993

(in lakhs)

Level	*SCs*				*STs*			
	Boys	*Girls*	*Total*	*Disparity Ratio*	*Boys*	*Girls*	*Total*	*Disparity Ratio*
Primary	104.1 (59.2)	71.7 (40.8)	175.8 (100.0)	1.45	51.5 (60.0)	34.4 (40.0)	85.9 (100.0)	1.47
Middle	35.7 (64.0)	20.1 (36.0)	55.8 (100.0)	1.78	14.2 (64.8)	7.7 (35.2)	21.9 (100.0)	1.84
Secondary/ Higher Secondary	19.8 (70.5)	8.3 (29.5)	28.1 (100.0)	2.39	6.8 (68.7)	3.1 (31.3)	9.9 (100.0)	2.19
Higher Education	2.9 (74.4)	1.0 (25.6)	3.9 (100.0)	2.89	0.9 (69.2)	0.4 (30.8)	1.3 (100.0)	2.25

Table 2.14: Dropout Rates for the Years 1980-81 to 1993-94 (in percentages)

(in percentages)

Year	Classes I-V			Classes I-VIII			Classes I-X		
	Boys	Girls	Total	Boys	Girls	Total	Boys	Girls	Total
1980-81	56.20	62.50	58.70	68.00	79.40	72.70	79.80	86.63	82.46
1981-82	51.10	57.30	53.50	68.50	77.70	72.10	79.44	86.81	82.33
1982-83	49.40	56.30	52.10	66.04	74.96	69.57	78.21	86.24	81.37
1983-84	47.83	53.96	50.26	66.10	75.27	69.26	76.41	84.79	79.71
1984-85	45.62	51.41	47.93	61.83	70.86	65.39	74.71	83.34	78.13
1985-86	45.84	50.27	47.61	60.70	70.04	64.42	73.97	83.16	77.62
1986-87	46.87	51.17	48.60	61.44	70.16	64.90	73.27	81.33	76.44
1987-88	43.28	49.42	46.97	58.80	67.55	62.29	72.14	80.06	75.30
1988-89	46.74	49.69	47.93	59.38	68.31	65.40	72.68	79.46	75.36
1989-90	46.50	50.35	48.08	61.00	68.75	64.09	70.99	77.72	73.66
1990-91	40.10	45.97	42.60	59.12	65.13	60.91	67.50	76.95	71.34

(Contd.)

Table 2.14 (*Contd.*)

Year	*Classes I-V*			*Classes I-VIII*			*Classes I-X*		
	Boys	*Girls*	*Total*	*Boys*	*Girls*	*Total*	*Boys*	*Girls*	*Total*
1991-92	41.03	45.17	42.78	54.30	62.04	57.48	68.55	75.87	71.51
1992-93	40.07	43.02	41.30	53.99	60.06	56.48	6815	74.69	70.80
1993-94	30.07	39.05	37.32	49.95	56.78	52.80	68.41	74.54	70.90

Note: Dropout rate is calculated as follows:

For Example: Year 1980-81

(i) Classes I-V = $\frac{\text{(No. of students enrolled in class I in 1976-77)} - \text{(No. of students in class V in 1980-81)}}{\text{No. of students enrolled in 1976-77}} \times 100$

(ii) Classes I-VIII = $\frac{\text{(No. of students enrolled in class I in 1973-74)} - \text{(No. of students enrolled in class VIII in 1980-81)}}{\text{No. of students enrolled in class I in 1973-74}} \times 100$

(iii) Classes I-X = $\frac{\text{(No. of students enrolled in class I in 1971-72)} - \text{(No. of students enrolled in class X in 1980-81)}}{\text{No. of students enrolled in class I in 1971-72}} \times 100$

This ration does not include: (i) Repeaters and (ii) Children entering the system after class I.

Source: Department of Education, Ministry of Human Resource Development, New Delhi, 1995.

The table shows that within a period of 14 years 1980-81 to 1993-94 the dropout ratios in three stages, primary, middle and secondary have decreased. While the dropout rate for class I-V was about 59 per cent, for class I-VIII was around 73 per cent and for class I-X was 82 per cent in 1980-81, allowing only 18 students to reach class X, in 1993-94 after 14 years the dropout rate stood 37 per cent, 53 per cent and 71 per cent respectively allowing only 29 students to reach class X. So for class I-X is concerned the decrease of dropout rate between 1980-81 and 1993-94 has been 13.41 per cent not so conspicuous. The table reflects that in all years dropout rates for girls have been higher than those for boys.

Thus, we have miles to go in achieving the universal elementary education (UEE) as enshrined in our Constitution as also to bridge the rural, urban, male, female, scheduled caste and scheduled tribes and non SC/ST categories. Improvement of literacy is the first step towards the formation of human capital because it lays down the foundations on which a better education pyramid can be erected. The definition of 'literacy' as given by the census of 1991 seems to be very weak. The census (1991) applied the yardstick of whether one could read but not write was not treated as a literate. This definition did not insist on the minimum number of years of schooling or a minimum knowledge of numeracy. But the Government of India would not like to evolve a stricter definition of literacy because that would on the one hand, demonstrate a poor-literacy show (poorer than what is shown today) and on the other cost much larger expenditure and effort to achieve the objectives of Universal Elementary Education, cutting across the large percentage of dropout rates at various levels of educational pyramid.

3

DYNAMICS OF TEACHING AND TESTING

Teaching has been a unique and noble trend all through the ages cutting across impediments in the form of bias and prejudices. Society always has been rendering it a fresh touch with itself undergoing a metamorphosis. Teaching in response, has intermittently tried to change its characteristics underlying according to the dynamics of society. It has always found itself at a flux throwing away bold challenges to its contemporary obtuse moorings, obscurities and statistics. It has proved its universalities embracing all sections of the society irrespective of their caste, creed, sex and religion, and its nobleness taking the most precious formative and impressionable years of human life into its fold; and has gained momentum at several angles of human existence. Hence teaching has become all pervasive, humanity-oriented and the teacher its carer, preserver and upholder.

The present world situation is as much a challenge to statesmen as to teachers who are in a happy position to influence thousands of young minds. But before anything gets done, teachers have to educate themselves first of all particularly the category of teachers that has been brought up on the values of closed or aggressive nationalism has to be taught out of its narrow outlook. The position in regard to the rising generation of teachers is somehow fortunate for it has in its heritage, a larger share of world-consciousness. Training of teachers for promoting the cause of world citizenship is inescapable logic of the situation and a good part of the destiny of humanity rests on how this business is done. A few points that follow in regard to the education of children and the youth apply more or less to the training of teachers.

Along with family, elementary schools are the places where children build their patterns of life. It is here that they have early, but of far-reaching influence, experiences. The potentiality of these schools for helping build society is generally not sufficiently realised as yet. Social processes of vie and take common play and the rest that go on in those schools lay the foundations of much-needed virtue of healthy adjustability with fellow beings. It is one of the most important functions of primary school teachers not only to help children develop healthy group loyalty but to see that the sphere of this loyalty is gradually extended to larger and larger groups.

Play, common, hobbies dinners and such like experiences can be easily availed of by teachers for fostering the community spirit among children. They can be encouraged to develop pen-friendship with children of other countries as well as exchange gift packages with them. Stories of children and details of the flora and fauna of other lands can also be profitably narrated by the teachers in the service of international understanding. Vital experiences of international sympathy should be kept alive in the minds of children through interesting narratives and films. On occasions of national importance children of the schools of one country may be led to send greetings to those of the other, so that another channel of international is opened.

The small children do not understand the language of tough reason and logic. They live mostly in the world of emotional and sentimental experiences. Their sentiments have therefore to be nourished very carefully. Happy experiences of childhood are a lasting asset of any society. Hence, teachers should see that the children under their charge derive happy moments of life by inter-personal and intergroup relations. Boredom, anxiety, fear or any other form of personality deficiency, is bound to escape in to dangerous results. Chances are heavy that those who lack adjustments in early childhood generally remain misanthropes throughout life and cause conflicts, small or great as their sphere of activities may permit. Generally, rules of mental and moral hygienes need be properly appreciated by teachers and put into practice so that the happy world of children grows without break into a happy world of adults, free from enervating conflicts and devastating wars.

Moreover, attitudes have a profound influence or human behaviour. Bulk of our attitudes is picked up ready-made from our cultural environments. Therefore, it becomes the serious concern of the teachers to see that undesirable attitudes do not go unchallenged. The psychology and sociology of attitudes should therefore figure prominently in the curriculum of teacher training, institutions. Right attitudes have a way of getting social difficulties solved out, while wrong attitudes may make the world look upside down. At school and college levels favourable attitudes for national and world unit should be built with all the means at the disposal of the teachers.

Teaching Methods

Some of the helpful methods may be considered.

1. *Right Information*

Right and adequate information serves as an efficacious corrective to prejudices and at times, to aggressive behaviour. Informing and reforming go hand in hand and it is just fair that people all over the world share common information based on truth. Papers and magazines suiting the academic level of students as cover items of cultural and material contributions of one country to the other, whether presently or in the past, deserve generous welcome into school and college libraries. Teachers can lead the young children to the habit of collecting clipping of such material for wall display along with their pictorial streamlining round the material. Besides, young things should be encouraged through the inspiration of teachers and through early available material to piece together various points of information on how children and grown-ups live their lives in different countries.

Passing of wrong information to the students by the teachers inside the classroom may lead the former to a false directions and may in the long run, spoil the student teacher relationship. It is therefore, the responsibility of the teachers, as torch bearers of truth, to properly enlighten their students. Wallpapers and Daily News Boards could well be utilised to this end alongside the teachers skill to convey news and views informally.

2. *Face-to-Face Contacts*

Amongst the factors that build healthy sentiments of friendship, face-to-face contacts are easily the most weighty when people work together for a common cause they normally develop bonds of the close association. Such contacts, by and large, help break the rigid isolationism of individuals and groups by removing their imaginary grievances, fears and suspicions regarding one another. Within the bounds of educational theory and practice, this principle is being usefully employed. Camps should be organised often involving students and teachers from various regions for common living and common work. This occasion becomes quite informative and skill-testing for the students as well as for the teachers. Here narrow parochialism or the trivial self slides into national consciousness or into the larger issues of humanity.

In a vast country like ours which has yet to grow into a fully unified nation, exchange of teachers and students between universities should prove of great consequence.

Study tours, even of a few weeks duration, have a profound effect in enlarging human understanding and sympathy. By providing first hand observation, personal contacts and group discussions they will prove to be life-transforming experiences. There is, therefore, a point in what Hazlitt says, "With change of place we change our ideas; nay, our opinions and feelings (Prem Nath: 293).

In toto, face-to-face contacts bring about close co-operation among the teachers and students and the latter get more informations about a topic because of cross-conversational interpretations. Moreover, they help the participants in gaining new insights and new concepts as the result of their cross-sectional and cross-regional contacts.

3. *The Curriculum*

In keeping with the rising social order towards one world, the school and university curricula hold be given healthy re-orientation. Although generally the curricula should not be rigid and indoctrinating, yet they should have enough of potentialities for reconditioning the minds of children and youth in favour of nationalism and internationalism.

Study of comparative religions has to be included in the curricula of the school and university education. Because of adverse conditioning they wallow in their perverted religious practices to the utter neglect of the universal religious spirit which teaches the fatherhood of God and brotherhood of man. In this scientific and technological age there seems a great ease for introducing the study of comparative religions in all stages of our education. Days of all great religious leaders should be celebrated without discrimination collaborated without discrimination and their preachings impressed upon pupils judiciously.

All in all, the aim of educational programme found religions should be to create religious spirit in the minds of the educands. It is the universal aspect of religions which should be presented by the curricula and religious practices.

Teaching of Geography and History, in this age, also needs a great deal of reorientation. Facts and events relating to both the subjects should be presented in the larger perspective of mankind in preference to regional and sectional framework. While referring to geographical facts, for instance, the Geography teacher can explain the interdependence of countries in the matter of agricultural products how food per necessity has to be rushed from the surplus areas to the deficit areas, and so on. The International School of Geneva has broken the traditional practice of teaching Geography. Instead of presenting to students regional and national maps first, it seeks to familiarize them with the global maps at the very outset and then coming down to the regional and national maps later. This does have an impression on the minds of the students to the effect that their own land is just a tiny part of the globe and in so many ways they are dependent on different regions of the world (Nath: 295).

Similarly, history should be interpreted to the advantage of international harmony. It should be possible to prove in the context of history that wars and other international conflicts are not unavoidable biological necessities, as some people maintain, but are precisely the conditions created by groups of men. The causes of war, the rise of great personality into power politics and the down fall of great empires etc., should be explained with critical analysis—economic factors, religious and political fanaticism, fear and distrust should be spotlighted as some of the major causes of the major international and national events. While teaching history, the perspective of the teacher should be nothing short of humanity notwithstanding the focus on national history.

The study of civics and political science at different stages of school and college programmes should be similarly broad-based. Which conveying to students the outlines of citizenship, a teacher in civics should be able to broaden the concept to that of the citizenship of the world. Loyalties, rights and duties should not be shown to attach to national boundaries only but to the whole world as well.

Political Science, as a subject should not limit itself in a narrow way to the study and problem of individual actions but, true to the spirit of science, should embrace wider range of topics, like the international politics and economy, and above all, international ethics to which the former ought to be subordinated. Current problems of vital consequences to the world, such as atomic energy, nuclear fission and bacteriological warfare, should be studied with their positive and negative sides.

Literature likewise, should not loom as a dull matter of grammatical rules and verbal compositions. It should be negotiated more creatively so as to yield living emotions and high values bordering on humanism and world brotherhood. Like philosophy it should be taught as a great cultural discipline which does not only convey facts and opinions but generates, in a gracious way the finer and noble feelings which the real meaning to human relationship and existence.

Besides the technical aspects of science, the study of science should be conceived in the background of the social needs and aspirations of humanity. Cultural aspects and consequence of science should form an integral part of the modern school curriculum. The objective should be to cultivate the scientific attitude embracing the qualities of impartiality, patience and industry in search of truth. Scientific discoveries, inventions and adventures with their stupendous contributions to the mankind should form the main components of the study of science.

In a country like India education can only develop the child into a functional citizen. This of course will be accomplished through development of right type of curriculum and its proper implementation. The constitutional directive however, so far has remained a mere dream because we are still far from the target. An analysis of the enrolment pattern has revealed that most of the uncovered population belongs to weaker sections—scheduled caste, scheduled tribes and women.

One of the reasons responsible for backlog of children belonging to weaker sections relates to curriculum (G.L. Arora: 22). It is observed that the curriculum is not relevant to their needs, it is biased in favour of middle class beneficiaries. There have been several attempts towards making the curriculum, more relevant, more relevant to local specific needs of the children in general and children of weaker sections in particular. Basic education profounded by Mahatma Gandhi and operationalised by Dr. Zakir Hussain provided a need based curriculum relevant to the community. The system was adopted as the national system in the post-Independence era. The system had to be abolished due to public pressure and vested interests. The basis of criticism was that the system is discriminatory in the sense that the population served by it will remain backward due to increased emphasis on productive activity, community activity and integrated approach to curriculum, since this will reduce weightage of academic curriculum meant for the privileged group.

Another attempt was made to prepare differential curriculum in Science and Mathematics for the students with varied backgrounds, needs and aspirations which also earned the same criticism. It is, therefore, evident from the reaction to the differential, need based curriculum for weaker sections that they themselves are not favourably inclined to the adoption of a differentiated curriculum. This is a significant issue which needs serious consideration.

4. *Bulletin Boards*

Bulletin boards and teaching displays serve various important functions. When only one copy of a useful resource is on hand it can be displayed on the board. The jackets of books, displayed, sometimes may encourage reading. Problems presented in bulletin boards or teaching displays may be studied and discussed by student groups as a part of class activity. A class may be divided into small groups to prepare bulletin boards or displays that review main ideas studied or that summarise information related to specific instructional objectives.

5. *Chalk Board*

Most competent teachers make special efforts to use the chalk board effectively. For lesson elements that develop from simple to complex ideas for example they build their explanations on chalk board point by point. They add symbols, charts, maps or outlines at just the right time to emphasise the content involved. Chalk board work permits immediate feedback information on both accuracy of work and knowledge of procedures. Students also can do practice work directly on the board. Some solve arithmetic problems while others work at desks. When the chalk board is used for student or teacher presentation, a few technique should be remembered.

a) The chalk board should not be crowded with too much matter. A few important points make vivid impression.

b) The work on chalk board should be planned in advance.

c) Lighting conditions should be checked. Glare should be avoided.

d) Writing on the board should be large enough to be visible at a distance.

6. *Overhead Projector*

The overhead projector has wide acceptance at all levels of teaching. Most teachers and students recognise the advantages of overhead projection techniques. Over head projector transparencies are also popular because they permit a,high degree of creativity in the preparation and presentation of ideas, both verbal and visual. With transparencies the teacher may use a number of methods in a colorful sequence to present ideas up to the students satisfaction. The teacher may take advantage of many opportunities to use them to create suspense and surprise and to stimulate student attention. Using such transparencies in teaching will be rewarding in communicating ideas and in encouraging the participation of every student in the class.

7. Slide Projector

Slides are projected by an instrument equipped with a powerful light source in a lamp house and carriers for holding slides of suitable size. It is a simple mechanism and the essential elements in it are the same as in filmstrip projector. The projectors can be operated by remote control. It is possible to record the narration in a tape-record and the later may be hooked up to the projector in such a way as to give the necessary commentary without the help of the teacher.

8. Filmstrip Projector

A filmstrip is a piece of non-inflammable safety film 35 mm wide varying in length up to about one meter. It is a related sequence of transparent still pictures and may contain from 10 to 50 pictures of frames. These pictures may be a connected series of drawings, photographs, diagrams or combination of these. The advantage of using filmstrip are as follows:

a) Usually a projected image draws the attention of the audience;

b) Varieties of information may be given. However, the effectiveness of the filmstrip depends in a large measure upon the still of the teacher. Now filmstrips with commentary recorded on tapes are available. The teachers can also tape this comments and play the tape synchronising it with the frame of the filmstrip.

c) The cost of the projector is comparatively low.

9. Radio

The radio plays and important role in imparting instruction to school children. Educational broadcasts based on curriculum are made on specific days at specific school hours, mainly for the benefit of the educational institutions. Booklets describing the details of programmes of educational broadcasts for the year are prepared and printed in advance by All India Radio and made available to educational institutions at the beginning of the academic year. Programmes are arranged separately for the benefit of elementary, middle and high schools and for university correspondence course students. The teacher as per the programmes can make necessary arrangements and create favourable learning situation. An evaluation report on any specific broadcasting based on the feedback and results of completed assignments and projects by students can be prepared by the teacher and sent to AIR. This will help the programmers to plan better programmes or presentation differently.

10. Tape Recorder

The tape recorder can be used to record educational broadcasts and for replay at suitable and convenient times. It can be used to record music and other sound effects for us during stage production of dramas of schools and cultural performances. It can also be used to record the talks of important persons which can be used later. In teacher training in estimations, a tape recorder is effectively used during the micro teaching sessions. The tape recorder provides the necessary feedback for discussions to improve the lesson.

11. Television

The word television represents different things to different people. In education, there are many interpretations of what television is. Television technology permits trans-mission of live programmes or motion pictures by cable, microwave, instructional, fixed stationery items, satellite or conventional broadcasting to schools or colleges or other institutions to view instructional programmes live or to record them for subsequent use. Students benefit from a variety of materials of educational value derived from programmes that they view at home.

A good teacher encourages students to view well produced programmes presented after school hours. A teacher should take trouble to look at the various programmes. A teacher knows students likes and dislikes and hence can help them to discover values in different programmes. This is one of the challenges and it is the duty of the teacher to be a bridge between the television viewing voice of his students and their work in the classes.

12. Computer

Computer Assisted Instruction (CAI) is a very effective method of learning. There are three general approaches to the integration of computer technology into instructional media. First, the computer can be used as an instrument of instruction in its own right. Second, it can be integrated with other instructional resources to produce sophisticated learning systems. Third, it can be absorbed into other media thereby producing equipment that is easier to use, safer and more reliable.

The computer has several distinct over more conventional instruction media. These include its almost unlimited storage capacity (memory), its accurate and rapid retrieval of information, its problem solving capacity and its versatility in terms of possible modes of presentation.

Basically CAI system includes a computing centre together with a number of student terminals. Typically the learner interacts with the computer programme by means of a type writer keyboard and/or a video screen that reacts to a light pen. The machine in turn communicates with the learner via audio and/or video system.

Computers are not widely used in education, particularly as instructional systems. This is partly because of lack of instructional (programme) and partly because computers are expensive. Still, if it is used it provides larger utility in comparison to the other teaching methods.

Teacher and Value Inculcation

The National Policy on Education, 1986 begins its sections on 'The Teacher' with a very comprehensive and meaningful statement, "The status of the teacher reflects the socio-cultural ethos of a society, it is said that no people can rise above the level of their teachers". It further expects the government and the community to create conditions that would motivate and inspire teachers on constructive and creative lines. The aptness of the policy formulations is beyond question and the same is reinforced by the fact that when this policy was revised in 1992 not a single word was changed in this particular paragraph (Inderpal Singh: 57).

Unfortunately, whenever a reference is made to the poor learning environment in schools, the blame is invariably put on the teacher, his irregularity, unpreparedness and unwillingness to perform the assigned tasks. This approach has not changed visibly as get in spite of several initiatives launched in pursuance of the 1986 policy. During the recent times, greater attention has been focussed on the quality of school education and learner attainments, particularly in elementary education. The Education Commission (1964-66) had observed, "of all the factors that influence the quality of education ... the quality, competence the character of teachers are undoubtedly the most significant." These attributes listed as most desirable by the Kothari Commission are obviously dependent upon and closely linked to the quality of initial teacher training in-service education and other professional and technical support made available to the teacher. To strengthen teacher training programmes several District Institutes of Education and Training (DIETs), Colleges of Teacher Education (CTEs) and Institutes of Advanced Studies in Education (IASEs) have been established throughout India. A lot has been attempted, much more still needs to be accomplished.

How shall we develop the quality and character of the teachers? The basic mandate of education is to prepare the young persons for future. The level of fulfilment of such expectations would be an outcome of the level of application, understanding and action on part of the teachers.The quality and character of teachers can hardly be developed by providing them education and training in cognitive areas alone. Far more needs to be done particularly in terms of inculcating and internalising humanistic, ethical and moral values amongst the young teachers. What matters most is not what is taught but, more importantly, how its taught.

The industrial, electronic and informational revolutions have opened new vistas of progress and development. It has also led to global concern for inculcation of values through education. The visible impact of science and technology is that of materialistic development at a very fast pace. The educational scene is India is changing fast. The liberalisation has its impacts in several spheres of educational endeavours. The foreign funding in elementary education is a major development of the recent past. The implications and impacts of educational change are to be watched carefully in years to come. The fruits and gains are not getting distributed evenly. Ends are considered more important than means. Concern for others gets diminished in the process. No section including teachers can remain aloof from such over-powering trends.

Hence, institutions and enlightened individuals should get into an analysis to ensure that universally accepted values and norms continue to guide the path of younger generations in schools, colleges and universities. This could not be done by including few chapters in the text books, providing separate text books or by earmarking one or two periods per week in the time table. Any suggestion at this juncture that schools colleges, universities must undertake the responsibility to ensure imparting of universal values of love and affection, caring for others and welfare of the society could be taken as a rhetoric by many. This may not be the case. Institutions narrated by dedicated and self-effacing individuals have always played outstanding role in transferring societies and communities.

The need of the hour is to repose faith in the teachers and the institutions. The two together if allowed to perform as per their own strategies should certainly be able to perceive and visualise what is best for the young persons under their charge. The extent of influence which a teacher casts upon the children is well known and understood. The teacher is the role model for the children and what they imbibe gets multiplied subsequently in the society. One most understand fully the impact that a teacher even in a remote primary school creates through his pupils after 10 years, 15 years or 20 years in the society.

Talking of teachers and the multiplying effects of their work one must immediately revert to the teacher training institutions. The number of teachers they produce has a direct relevance to the multiplier effect that is likely to be visible in the society. The curricular of teacher training institutions has not ignored value inculcation and this does find a place in the curriculum. Even such questions are to be answered as 'how values can be inculcated.' What usually gets ignored is the fact that value inculcation must permeate all sectors of society and all such activities that influence the family and society. It must also be understood that education alone can not be held totally responsible for value inculcation. Parents community and society must also accept their respective roles and responsibilities. The teacher training institutes could definitely consider implementing such strategies which require more effort, initiative, foresight and commitment and not financial inputs of a very large magnitude.

The teacher educators, while preparing the teachers could focus on developing strategies that would enable critical examination of every content unit from the point of view of developing views and ethics. The learner-teacher interaction which has become a rare commodity has been found to be much more effective in passing on the experience of the older generation to the younger generation. Regularity and availability of teachers in institutions during working hours makes a big difference. The teacher has to be the nodal point. An interactive environment nurtures willingness to learn and to internalise more and more. It has been the experience of may heads of institutions that group activities and participatory programme like dances, dramas, sports, national integration campaign become much effective when staff members also participate and enliven the total learning environment.

Alternative role model, other than the teachers is not easily in evidence. After Independence one could easily identify persons of integrity, sacrifice and an aura of others than themselves, their families or relations. They enjoyed tremendous respect from the younger generation. Not many of them are with us now. Institutions can still strive and arrange interactions with man of letters and scholarship, creative talents and those known for their sense of devotion and dedication. While organising activities in institutions it has to be ensured that in all programmes, celebrations, gatherings and significant occasions no religious or cultural group is neglected or isolated. The institutional response to emergency situations like floods, fire, drought also make learners realise the need for cooperative action and combined efforts in life. At the time of natural calamities young students and student leaders, if tackled caringly by the teachers would show the best within them. In toto, a long term, sustained and nationwide effort needs to begin from institutions of teacher training to revive the process of value inculcation in the present context and develop responsible, skilled and motivated young persons to shoulder the responsibilities for the future.

Teacher-training at the level of higher education is no longer in the conceptual stage. Gone are the days when the teachers of universities and colleges used to treat their institutions as citadels and private preserves with a sign "Trespassers will be prosecuted". Teaching skill is no longer something sacred and esoteric nor is it any more looked upon as part of an individual's natural endowment or genetic equipment. It is admitted on all hands today that teaching is a public activity and a trainable skill. No doubt, universities have reconciled themselves to the idea of 'orientation course' and 'refresher courses' for the college and university teachers.

In recent time there has been a change in the thinking of educators who begin to think that teacher training is necessary. Reasons are:

(a) the structure of education has become a mass production operation;

(b) towering personalities and role models whose example could be followed have become obsolete if not extinct as a species;

(c) the multifarious tasks including teaching, tutorials and seminars valuation of scripts and assignments, counselling extra curricular and co-curricular activities have made it necessary for the teacher to acquire certain skills and expertise;

(d) the student is no longer the empty vessel into which learning can be poured. He is no longer the willing clay in the hands of the lecturer to be moulded as the latter pleased. Explosion of knowledge and population followed by implosion of values and erosion of disciplines have imposed new demands on the college teachers. There is, therefore, increasing awareness of the complex nature of the tasks to be performed by him and his responsible role as change agent in a democratic society.

(e) modern technology has shifted emphasis from 'teaching' to 'learning'.

If the teacher doesn't keep his knowledge upto-date with commensurate re-tooling of his professional skill, the teacher loses his influence and becomes obsolete. Hence a teacher is an academic specialist, a methodologist, a character trainer of pupils, and effective members of the school staff and an effective member of the society.

For the all round success of the students in particular and society in general teaching is not the only area where much attention has to be focussed upon. Students' responsibility in terms of reading, learning and writing is too a greater area to be cultivated often. Some of the points on reading techniques may be discussed here.

Reading Techniques

Writing ability follows reading ability. Men learn by what they read, not by dictionaries or manuals. A style begins as an invitation of other people's styles and grows into an expression of the writer's own mind and personality. Memorising a book of rules does not produce a good writer. Although every writer should know the rules of grammar, some acquire knowledge of structure and grammar indirectly and inductively, subconsciously preceiving structure in the material and making the required generalisations. Therefore, one should read extensively and intensively.

So far higher education is concerned it should create in the students mind the desire and the habit of coming to his own independent conclusions after reading as many books and journals as available, and carefully considering the different points of view. He should have first hand contact with the great ideas contained in the books and conveyed by outstanding thinkers. For this purpose, it is necessary to cultivate reading habits and receive systematic training in reading which is not a natural faculty or a casual activity. Unfortunately, today's students read little beyond materials that are required for their courses or the examinations. In fact, they read limited materials likely to be useful for their final examination which leads to the award of a degree. As students of undergraduate classes are immature they need to be guided in reading. The improvement of the students' reading habits is the responsibility of the entire teaching staff. As each subject has its specific requirements and needs different techniques each faculty member has to design his own strategy and provide expert advice to the student.

Good reading functions in two areas: 1) Selection of books and reading materials; and 2) Methods of study or employment of suitable reading techniques. Here lies the most important responsibility of the teachers. The teacher has to give them all the help and direction in reading. To an inexperienced and immature student all the books and contents of the books appear to be equally important. He believes in the sanctity of the printed word and he can not organise the material in logical sequence and fit it into the framework of the relevant conclusions without proper guidance. Therefore, the teacher should help him with advice in taking notes and arranging the matter after careful and judicious selections of essential data/material.

Reading is not a casual activity or birthday gift. It is a skill. One needs systematic cultivation and constant care to acquire this complex skill. There are good books on this. In an expert an article "How to Read More Efficiently", Paul Leady said that a person should be able to read 600 to 1000 words per minute and remember 80 per cent of what is read (Chalapati Rao: 104). The students must be trained in the different kinds of reading for different purposes.

Carter Alexander and Irvid Burke, two scholars did research on reading and on the basis of their finding classified it under five categories:

1) Scanning :- A mechanical activity like checking a Telephone Directory or a Railway Time Table.

2) Scouting :- Searching or exploring for valuable references and determining their main features.

3) Skimming :- Very rapid or speed reading with a view to obtaining the key points or main ideas without seeking full details (Novels, short stories and narrative prose).

4) Reading Critically :- Grasping full meaning and problem solving or intensive reading (Reflectory and expository prose, criticism-tough poetry).

5) Interpreting :- The final and difficult stage of reading. Applying what is read to a conceptual framework or one's own problem (Abstract subject matter-critical prose-Epic poetry).

These relate to reading in general. But each subject has its special needs. With proper advice and supervision we can expect the students to exercise more judgement about book selection, to range more widely in the area of investigation and to contact original and stimulating books which are the sources of ideas that widen their mental horizons and enrich their lives. They will cultivate the habit of thinking and reacting to the perspectives presented in a book.

Tutorials and seminars are not spoon-feeding or exam-coaching sessions. They as instructional methods play an important role this field guided or assigned reading. The student is expected to read books or portions of books as directed by the teacher, prepare an exercise and defend it when it is criticised by steps in as a midwife or a catalytic agent to argument, contradictions or inconsistencies in the presentation or the language points. On the basis of this feedback the teacher can further guide his students reading. The teacher's role is not that of a formal authority. He is an expert, a midwife, a catalyst, an arbiter or moderator.

While focusing the student's attention on the specific requirements of the course the teacher should endeavour to stimulate and encourage other kinds of reading. In the hands of a good teacher the text is only a tool and the syllabus a minimum programme. The best results come only when the students reading is properly guided and interest is created to read innovative critical and path-breaking books and articles in journals. The teacher can achieve this in some specific ways. He may for example, make a special reference to a book or a portion of it to arouse interest. He may make a special point of mentioning quotations from a book or books that he himself has read. The teacher should give annotated bibliography or reading lists for individual judgement and selection by students. It encourages library exploration. The students scripts and assignments will be the basis for further guidance. Selected paragraphs and chapters in books may be used to teach them how to identify key points and (main) the central idea.

The success of the student in his examinations and his life in future depends upon the success of this programme of Guided Reading and Supervised Study which is an antidote to the universal but useless habit of memorising textbooks and blindly reproducing the contents.

Curriculum Design

Curriculum is often mistaken for syllabus. Curriculum design is not mere syllabus formulation. Syllabus is only a part of the curriculum in a narrow sense. Curriculum is the totality of the educational programmes which are planned to achieve certain purposes stated in general way. The objectives of a curriculum are formulated on the basis of the goals set by the society keeping in view the society's problems and needs. When the problems change the curriculum should change. But this does not happen always and everywhere. The curriculum is also modified when it is found that it has developed some deficiencies or defects which make it incapable for fulfilling the objectives.

Curriculum is a ground plan of action which sets the objectives of an educated system, defines the inputs that should go into it and specifies the outputs of terminal behaviour. Objectives are the quintessence of it. While fixing the specific objectives curriculum should also take care of the general development of the student. It is a set of practical directives for those who are guiding the learning process in educational institutions so that their guidance will be clear, effective and methodical.

Curriculum may be of two kinds—product-oriented which involves a finalised amount of knowledge or skills and process-oriented which stimulates an on-going and increasing learning process.

A curriculum design should have the following principles or elements:

Theoretical Method

1) A definition of goods of what the teacher wants the student to perform.
   a) General or final goals which will orient the learning process in the subject in terms of knowledge, attitudes and skills.
   b) Intermediate or strategic goals clearly explaining what is attainable within given time-frame and available means and capabilities and is relevant in the given social situation.
   c) Concrete targets as successive steps towards the intermediate goals.
2) The section of content through which knowledge skills and attitudes as required in the goals can be acquired and exercise.
3) Choice out of the available methods and operations to ensure most effective guidance (Lecture, Tutorial, Seminar etc.)
4) The selection of useful teaching materials and indication of how they can be used and improved.
5) Since teaching and testing are two sides of the coin of education, the manner in which the selected methods operations and teaching materials are to be evaluated, should be indicated. There should be clear guidelines for the testing of the students performance. (Essay, oral questions, short-answer questions, multiple-choice objective questions etc. are used to test the pupil's performance.

The curriculum is an instrument in the hands of the teachers as well as the pupils. Therefore, it is desirable to fill the gaps in the knowledge and skills of the teachers. For this purpose re-training of the teachers is essential. Apart from professional training there should be a systematic re-training. Student's behaviour, their motivation and learning potential are to be studied properly. This is essential for curriculum design. Without this explorative research, there can be no curriculum planning.

Whenever there is a proposal to introduce new subject matter or teaching material or testing procedure, supportive evaluation research is necessary. This is necessary even if the same curriculum is proposed to be continued after two or three years. The ideal place for conducting such research is an experimental institution connected with teacher training in the case of school education and a good college of education for school education. For higher education, Academic, Staff Colleges, attached to the universities may undertake this research with the help of specially trained university or college teachers.

According to experts the curriculum followed in most of the universities and other educational institutions in India are traditional and not objective oriented. Since the syllabus is framed on an ached basis they do not specify the abilities and skills to be developed in the learner, nor do they give any guidelines to the teacher with regard to the teaching methods and techniques to be followed and the testing procedures to be adopted. The only device that gives an idea about the depth to which the subject matter is to be dealt with is the final examination. Decline in academic standards can therefore be attributed to the fact that teaching is lecture-based, teacher-paced and examination oriented (Rao: 49).

A sound curriculum design should process through the following successive stages.

a) Diagnostic study of the needs of the individuals and the society.

b) Formulation of suitable objectives.

c) Selection and sequential organisation of subject matter or content.

d) Identification, selection and organisation of learning experiences.

e) Determination of strategies priorities and the methods and ways of doing it.

These different stages are related and inter dependent since each of them is a logical outcome of the preceding one.

Practical Method

A committee of the concerned teachers, potential employees and curriculum experts should be constituted to conduct a survey of the chosen curriculum area by collecting information about the types of jobs or tasks the learners are expected to carry out after they pass the examination and about other needs of the society. Until Independence even today most universities have been functioning in traditional isolation. Some of them have become cloistered centres with little knowledge of and less contact with the community which really supported them and their institutions. This dichotomy between the university and the community is largely responsible for the offening of purely literary and academic studies by these centres of higher education. Hence the widely held public opinion of the lack of social relevance in the syllabi and curricula of the universities.

For the purpose of survey the committee may use 1) a well designed questionnaire 2) actual observation of jobs and 3) interview techniques. A detailed analysis of the learners in respect of knowledge skills and attitudes.

Then the committee will select the content based upon the formulated objectives. Selection and organisation of the content will involve criteria like validity and significance in addition to the specified objectives. At this stage the committee has to decide on the various levels of development at which the content has to be studied. In the case of languages, controlled vocabulary and current usage are the chief guides especially in the designing the curriculum for the undergraduate classes.

Planning of the learning experiences (learning activities that are used to achieve objectives) is the next stage. It requires great skill. The planners should possess a competent knowledge, strategy to clarify concepts, problem solving and priority order of the desired attitudes.

Then the validity and soundness of the proposed curriculum has to be evaluated. One has to test whether the stipulated objectives tally with the actual achievements of the learner.

It has to be further tested whether the curriculum provides experiences which offer maximum opportunities for the different levels of learners to achieve the goals. There should be two types of tests: 1) Formative evaluation techniques like objective tests and short answer tests (to be used in the early stage) and 2) Summative evaluation techniques like essay, short answer and objective (to be used in the final stage when the curriculum is fully developed). These tests are intended to obtain the feedback information. The feedback obtained through summative evaluation will show whether the curriculum design is strictly in accordance with the stipulated objectives.

In any sound system of education teaching and testing are inseparable and equally important. If teaching is to be given much attention and made more effective, the system of examination—internal assessment, terminal examinations question paper setting and evaluation etc. should be made that much effective A striking balance between teaching brings about a serence academic atmosphere and helps develop a good class of students. But the evils of the present system are that teaching is lecture-dominated and testing is essay-dominated. Examination is no longer a passport to the students' academic brilliance. It has become a game of chance. The need of the hour is to implement new kind of scheme entirely soothing to the varying structure of the educational system.

Ultimately the emotional involvement of the teachers is essential for the successful working out of any new scheme. Any plan, however sound and desirable, will be reduced to a force if those who have to work it are not motivated. The individual is more important than the system since the individual has the power and potentiality to transfer the system. We have to place our trust in the teachers. If the salt itself loseth its savour, where with can it be salted?

4

ARUNACHAL PRADESH : AN OVERVIEW OF ITS EDUCATION SYSTEM

Arunachal Pradesh (hence Arunachal) is a thinly populated, vast, hilly region, lying approximately between 26°28′ and 29°31′ North latitude and 90°31′ and 97°30′ East longitude. It occupies an area of 83,743 Kilometres and is situated in the extreme north-eastern corner of India. The neighbouring countries surrounding Arunachal are Myanmar in the east, Bhutan in the west, Tibet and China in the north and its sister states of Assam and Nagaland in the south. In 1972, Arunachal, the erstwhile NEFA (North Easter Frontier Agency) ceased to be tribal area within the state of Assam and got an independent political status of a Union Territory. The name of the union territory of NEFA was formally changed to Arunachal Pradesh under the North Eastern Areas (Reorganisation) Act of 1972. In 1975, a Legislative Assembly was constituted for the union territory and on February 20, 1987, Arunachal attained statehood.

For administrative purpose, the state has been divided into 13 districts, namely, Tirap (01.09.65) Changlang (14.11.87), Lohit (01.09.65), Dibang Valley (01.06.80), East Siang (01.06.80), Upper Siang (12.05.95), West Siang (01.06.80), Upper Subansiri (01.06.80), Papum Pare (22.09.92), Lower Subasiri (01.06.80), East Kameng (01.06.80), West Kameng (01.06.80) and Tawang (06.10.84); 21 Subdivisions, 123 circles and 56 blocks. Matters related to a particular tribe or community are decided at the village level. Since 1967, the three tier Panchayati Raj System has been introduced in the state, Zilla Parishad at District level, Anchal Samity at Block level and Gram Panchayat at village level.

Special Features of the State

The population of Arunchal Pradesh according to the Census of 1991, is 8,64,558 comprising 4,65,004 males and 3,99,554 females. The population is predominantly tribal and of Indo-Mongoloid origin. Only 0.46 per cent of the State's population comprises scheduled castes. About 93.4 per cent of the population dwell in rural areas. The state is thinly populated and the density of population per sq. km. is 10. The districts of Tirap and Dibang Valley have the highest and the lowest density—36 persons per sq. km. and 3 persons per sq. m. respectively. There are about 22 major tribes and nearly 45 sub-tribes, speaking 50 different languages and dialects and adopting Assamese or Hindi as the lingua franca amongst the different tribes. The diverse and hostile climatic factors (its topography is full of mountain terrains whose heights vary from 1000 feet 14,000 feet) alongwith diversity amongst tribes, their remoteness of location, differences in traditions, customs and dialects and absence of a lingua franca solely of the typical Arunachal Pradesh brand makes the spread of education by the state education department a very challenging one. Yet much ground has been covered very fast within a few years by a team of brave and dedicated people in the department with a strong missionary zeal in their heart. The birth and death rates in the state are higher than those of India as a whole (Kapoor, Vadhera, Mazumdar: 10-11).

Education System

Literacy

The total population of the State being 8,64,558 as per 1991 census, the growth rate of population between 1981 and 1991 was 36.83. The sex ratio was 861 : 1000. Literacy rate of the state as per 1991 census was 41.59%. A comparative picture of literacy rates in the state from 1961 to 1991 is given in Table 4.1.

Table 4.1: Literacy Rates: 1961-1991

Year	*Age Group*	*Persons*	*Males*	*Females*
1961	5 years and above	7.13	12.24	1.24
1971	5 years and above	11.29	17.82	3.71
1981	7 years and above	25.54	35.11	14.01
1991	7 years and above	41.59	51.45	29.69

Source: Census of India 1991, Arunachal Pradesh, Series 3.

Distribution of literate population in various districts of Arunachal Pradesh is shown in Table 4.2.

Structure

The state adopted the 10+2+3 system of education in 1974 which comprises ten years of secondary education, two years of higher secondary education and three years of under-graduate education leading to Bachelor's degree in Arts (B.A.), Science (B.Sc.) or Commerce (B.Com.). After attaining the first degree by the age of 20 years, a graduate may pursue first graduate courses in Arts, Science or Commerce for two years or may join one year's teacher training course to obtain a B.Ed. degree.

After class XII Board Examination students are eligible to sit for the Joint Entrance Examination for admission to professional courses in Engineering/Medicine/Veterinary Sciences/B.Sc. (Agriculture)/Fishery etc. and after class X Board Examination for admission to diploma courses. Of the total seats allotted for various courses, 80 percent are for Arunachal students who receive stipends at government

Table 4.2: District-wise Literate Population

State/District	*Total Population1991*			*Literate Population 1991**					
	Persons	*Males*	*Females*	*Persons*	*%age*	*Males*	*%age*	*Females*	*%age*
Arunachal Pradesh	8,64,558	4,65,004	3,99,554	2,83,610	32.80	1,91,841	41.25	91,769	22.96
1. Tawang	28,287	15,338	12,949	6,830	24.14	5,094	33.21	1,736	13.40
2. West Kameng	56,421	30,966	25,455	25,585	36.48	13,696	44.22	6,889	27.06
3. East Kameng	50,395	25,689	24,706	10,490	20.81	7,765	30.22	2,725	11.02
4. Lower Subansiri	1,55,378	82,277	73,701	51,517	33.15	33,731	40.99	17,786	24.13
5. Upper Subansiri	50,086	26,823	23,263	15,443	30.83	10,441	38.92	5,002	21.10
6. West Siang	89,936	48,029	41,907	31,931	35.50	20,482	42.64	11,449	27.32
7. East Siang	99,643	53,542	46,101	35,166	35.29	22,776	42.53	12,390	26.87
8. Dibang Valley	43,068	24,087	18,981	15,885	36.88	11,093	46.05	4,792	25.24
9. Lohit	1,09,706	61,043	48,663	42,204	38.47	28,847	47.25	13,357	27.44
10. Changlang	95,530	51,291	44,239	32,031	33.52	22,067	43.02	9,964	22.52
11. Tirap	85,508	45,919	39,589	21,528	25.17	15,849	34.51	5,679	14.34

* Literates exclude children in age group 0-6 who are treated as illiterates.

Source: Census of India, 1991, Arunachal Pradesh Series 3, Pt. II A and B.

approved rates. Earlier after successful completion of these courses, students receiving stipends were required to execute a bond of surety which has been waived since 1990.

There is no provision for studying medicine, agriculture or engineering in Arunachal Pradesh. The state government sponsors candidates for different under-graduate and post-graduate medical and professional courses against the reserved quota allotted by different Indian universities for students of the state. Fine arts students are likewise sent for training to different art institutions in the country.

A few state department also run educational institutions such as two ITIs under the Department of Industries. Health Training Research Centre under the Department of Medicine, Gram Sevak Training Centre and the Farmer's Training Centre under the Department of Agriculture, Arunachal forest school under the Department of Forest and School of Veterinary Science and Animal Husbandry under the Veterinary Department. Apart from these, the administration sponsors candidates for training as Rangers, Deputy Rangers and Assistant Conservator of Forests at Barnihat in Meghalaya.

The Government of India has set up in cooperation with the North Eastern Council, a North Eastern Regional Institute of Science and Technology (NERIST) at Itanagar, to meet the development needs of the region comprising seven states, for whom, 70 per cent of the seats are reserved that is at the rate of 10 per cent each, while the remaining 30 per cent seats are filled up on the basis of merit.

Educational Institutions

At the time of Independence, there were only 2 Primary Schools in the state with an enrolment of 30 students. After Independence, steps were taken for development of education by setting up Education Department under an Education Officer in September, 1947. At that time the strategy adopted was for rapid expansion of general education with special emphasis on Universal Elementary Education (UEE). But due to inaccessible areas, inadequate funds and communication difficulties, the progress was slow. Only after Chinese aggression in 1962, a rapid expansion of education took place to bring the area at par with the rest of the country. Investment in general education for the state during the plan periods is shown in Table 4.3.

Table 4.3: Investment in Five Year Plans in General Education (1951-1997)

(Rs. in lakhs)

S. No.	*Plan*	*Outlay*	*Expenditure*
1.	First	41.81	19.97
2.	Second	50.00	43.32
3.	Third	82.37	84.97
4.	Fourth	205.18	196.89
5.	Fifth	623.74	415.33
6.	Sixth	2778.02	2634.82
7.	Seventh	7454.23	7202.66
8.	Eighth	15190.00	21870.23

Source: Teacher Education in Arunachal Pradesh (NCTE), New Delhi.

With the implementation of the five year plans and increase in investment in various plan periods there has been rapid growth of education in the state. Since special emphasis was laid on UEE, more than 70% of the total funds have been spent on Elementary Education.

For popularising education and attracting more children to schools from villages, inter-villages residential primary schools popularly known as I.V. were established in the centrally located place from 1957-58 to 1989-90. The basic concept of the I.V. School was that the school served the people of a group of villages for imparting primary education to their children who will stay in the attached hostels and the government will bear all expenditure. At present, there are 1876 I.V. Schools functioning in the state. But these schools lack paper infrastructure facilities like all-weather proof school and hostel buildings. The villagers constructed ordinary base type (OBT) Kachcha houses where the schools were initially started. Most of the schools are yet to be provided with weather proof school buildings, hostels and teacher's quarters. In addition to the I.V. Schools, Primary Schools were opened and many of them were upgraded to middle, secondary and higher secondary ones.

Presently the educational infrastructure of the state starts at the top with a full-fledged Ministry of Education followed by the Secretariat of Education and the two Directorates namely (i) Directorate of School Education and (ii) Directorate of Higher Education at the state level. Downwardly, this framework is decentralised upto the grassroots level through various institutions and offices. They are at present :

(a) University	:	01
(b) Degree College	:	07
(c) Sports School	:	01
(d) Higher Secondary Schools	:	61
(e) Secondary Schools	:	81
(f) Middle Schools	:	285
(g) Primary Schools	:	1398

Source: Directorate of Higher Education and School Education, Naharlagun, Arunachal Pradesh.

Though the growth of educational facilities continued to be slow till 1960, a noteworthy achievement was made there after as is shown in Table 4.4 which reveals a substantial rise in the number of institutions with annual growth rate† of 4.27 during the period 1975-76 to 1997-98.

Table 4.4: Number of Institutions: 1975-76 to 1997-98

Intitutions	*Number*				
	1975-76	*1980-81*	*1985-86*	*1990-91*	*1997-98*
Higher Secondary	22	14	24	45	61
Secondary	*	30	44	68	81
Middle	88	117	43	254	285
Primary	622	845	949	1122	1398
All Schools	732	1006	1060	1489	1825

* Included in Higher Secondary

Sources: (i) *Education in India,* vol. I, 1980-81 and 1985-86, Ministry of HRD, Department of Education, Govt. of India.

(ii) Selected Educational Statistics, 1990-91 Ministry of HRD, Department of Education, Govt. of India.

(iii) Teacher Education in Arunachal Pradesh, NCTE, New Delhi, 1998

†$R = \text{Antilog}\left[\frac{\log Pt - \log P0}{t-0}\right]^{-1}$ Where R is geometric rate of growth

Besides there is a State Institute of Education, a District Resource Centre for Adult education a District Resource Centre for Science Education and a District Institute of Education and Training. Proposal for opening a DIET for each district is in the process. In addition to the above, there are number of schools of repute run by the private organisations and non-governmental organisations such as the Donyi-Polo Mission, Ramakrishna Mission, Vivekananda Kendra Vidyalayas, B.K. Mission and Kendriya Vidyalayas etc. which serve the educational needs of the state.

The medium of instruction at all the stages of education and in all schools is English. Hindi is taught as a second language while Assamese or Sanskrit as third language since 1972-73 (Presently no Sanskrit or Assamese). All secondary and higher secondary schools are affiliated to the Central Board of Secondary Education (CBSE) and follow the syllabus prescribed by the NCERT and CBSE. Part-time correspondence courses are also available. Almost all schools of the state are co-educational. Students are provided with scholarships and stipends for higher studies at various institutions outside the state. Selected girl students are sent to 'Banasthali Vidyapita' in Rajasthan and other institutions in the country. Board examinations for classes V, VIII and XI are conducted by the Directorate of School Education whereas the annual examinations of the left over classes are conducted by the schools concerned.

The future plan of the Government is to consolidate the achievement made so far and expand and strengthen the network of education, training, supervision, monitoring, management etc. Improving as well as maintaining quality in education still remains a vital issue for the Government. In this regard, upgrading and strengthening of the State Institute of Education (SIE), opening of more District Institutes of Education and Training (DIETS) and equipping the department with trained personnel of high quality and efficiency remain crucial points.

Need based training of teachers, striking a balance between the needs of the state and the national equivalence, strategies to tackle the content load and improvement of the achievements and awareness in the various areas and emerging trends in education remain to be great challenges for the state, though considerable and appreciable amount of work has been accomplished in this regard by the Arunachal University, S.I.E., S.R.C., DRCSE, DIET and the Directorate of School Education and Higher Education either independently or in collaboration with NCERT, CIEFL, CIH, CBSE and similar other external agencies.

The most important educational event during the VII plan period was adoption of a National Policy on Education (NPE) in May 1986 and a detailed Programme of Action (POA) for implementation in August, 1986. The NPE and the POA placed renewed emphasis on the programmes for teachers education with a view to bringing out a revolutionary change in the education scenario of the whole country. With the onset of the Programme of Mass Orientation of School Teachers (PMOST) it was for the fist time in the country that different teacher education institutes got the opportunity to cover such a large number of teachers through inservice training programmes. Establishment of DIETs envisaged providing training and academic support to the elementary education (both formal and non-formal) and adult education groups at the district level.

The well organised structural framework of the Education Department devotes its whole-hearted energy mainly to the spread of Education to every nook and corner of the remote North East ensuring a minimum level of education for one and all as well as improving maintaining quality of education through its devoted and dedicated team of teacher of various grades. For this purpose, certain state level institutions of repute have been established to raise the qualitative standards of education by bringing in newly researched knowledge within the teachers and the taught to the new dimensions of teaching and learning through improved techniques and use of educational technology.

Though the SIE, DRCSE and SRC responsible for inservice education of the teachers and other functionaries are discharging their duty the arrangements do not seem to be sufficient booking to the huge strength of teachers working in the schools of the state. Realising this the state government has decided to open nine more DIETs in different districts in order to take up teacher education in a vigorous manner.

A glimpse of teacher-pupil ratio at different stage and for different districts of the State is given in Table 4.5. It is 1:43 at primary school level, 1:17 at middle, 1:13 at secondary, 1:41 at higher secondary, 1:22 at college and 1:9 at the university stages.

Table 4.6 shows the enrolment of students at various stages during 1975-76 to 1995-96 and reveals that compared to the total student enrolment, percentage of enrolment of girls from 1975-76 to 1995-96 was low at all stages of education and it remained the lowest particularly at the secondary/higher secondary levels in 1995-96, i.e. 37% compared to its percentage of 44 at primary and 42 at middle school levels. The growth rate of enrolment at all stages in case of boys as well as girls was the highest during 1976-81. However, over the years from 1975-76 to 1980-81 the annual growth rate remains the least for both boys and girls in classes I-V and the highest in classes IX to XI/XII. The annual growth rates of both boys and girls at primary level are 2.8 and 6.17 respectively. This sort of rate of annual growth over the years of the enrolment at primary stage is surely going to affect the goal of Universalisation of Elementary Education (UEE) of the state. Serious efforts are needed to increase the student enrolment not only at the primary level but also at different stages of education since the annual growth rates of both boys and girls over the years too seem to be very discouraging at middle and secondary/higher secondary levels.

Table 4.7 shows that compared to the national average at all stages of school education, the number of pupils per teacher is lower at the state level. This may be attributed to its sparse population.

Table 4.8 which shows detailed statistics on teachers during the mid-seventies to early nineties, reveals that during a period of twenty years i.e., from 1975-76 to 1995-96 there has been a substantial rise with growth rate of 8.0 in the number of teachers in Arunachal Pradesh.

Table 4.5: Teacher-Pupil Ratio by Districts (1996-97)

Sl. No.	*State/ District*	*Teacher-Pupil Ratio*					
		Primary	*Middle*	*Secondary*	*Higher Secondary*	*College*	*University*
	Arunachal Pradesh	1:49	1:17	1:13	1:41	1:22	1:9
1.	Tawang	1:32	1:10	1:6	1:4		
2.	West Kameng	1:39	1:20	1:9	1:1	1:14	
3.	East Kameng	1:75	1:11	1:8	1:5		
4.	Lowar Subansiri	1:130	1:31	1:11	1:14		
5.	Upper Subansiri	1:57	1:19	1:16	1:5	1:30	
6.	Papum-Pare	1:43	1:16	1:25	1:6		1:9
7.	West Siang	1:49	1:15	1:14	1:3	1:45	
8.	East Siang	1:30	1:16	1:14	1:4	1:19	
9.	Upper Siang	1:46	1:20	1:36	1:1		
10.	Dibang Valley	1:87	1:11	1:19	1:3		
11.	Lohit	1:37	1:24	1:12	1:4	1:18	
12.	Chapglang	1:63	1:82	1:11	1:2	1:21	
13.	Tirap	1:39	1:18	1:13	1:2		

Source: Directorate of School Education, Arunachal Pradesh, Naharlagun.

Table 4.6: Enrolment of Students by Stages: 1975-76 to 1995-96

Stage	*Enrolment*					*Annual Growth Rate*			
	1975-76	*1980-81*	*1985-86*	*1990-91*	*1995-96*	*1976-81*	*1981-86*	*1986-91*	*1991-96*
Classes I-V									
Total	36344	59904	85132	112197	141904	10.15	7.64	5.19	5.19
Girls	10342	20129	33742	47154	63122	14.28	10.66	7.15	6.17
	(28)	(34)	(40)	(42)	(44)				
Boys	26002	39775	51390	65043	78782	9.41	5.19	4.71	2.80
Classes VI-VII									
Total	3121	8887	16241	26089	38189	23.02	13.24	9.64	8.14
Girls	732	2645	5961	10133	16215	29.41	17.49	11.17	10.15
	(23)	(30)	(37)	(39)	(42)				
Boys	2389	6242	10280	15956	21974	21.33	10.66	9.14	6.65
Classes IX-XI/XII									
Total	1112	4001	8834	15696	22363	29.14	16.94	12.20	7.15
Girls	182	921	2561	5008	8188	38.03	22.46	14.29	10.66
	(16)	(23)	(29)	(32)	(37)				
Boys	930	3080	6273	10688	14175	27.05	15.34	11.17	6.16

Note: Figures in parentheses denote percentage of girls in total.

Sources: (i) Education in India, Vol. I, 1975-76, 1980-81 and 1985-86, Ministry of HRD, Department of Education Govt. of India,
(ii) Selected Educational Statistics, 1990-91, Ministry of HRD, Department of Education, Govt. of India, 1992,
(iii) Teacher Education in Arunachal Pradesh, NCTE, New Delhi, 1998.

Table 4.7: Average No. of Pupils Per Teacher by Institutions: 1975-76 to 1990-91

Institution	*Average No. of Pupils per Teacher*			
	1975-76	*1980-81*	*1985-86*	*1990-91*
Higher Secondary	19 (25)	22 (26)	23 (29)	21 (32)
Secondary	*	21 (28)	22 (29)	24 (31)
Middle	22 (30)	19 (33)	22 (35)	21 (37)
Primary	30 (38)	28 (38)	32 (42)	29 (42)

* Included in Higher Secondary.

Note: Figures in parentheses denote teacher-pupil ratio at national level.

Sources: (i) *Education in India,* Vol. I, 1975-76, 1980-81 and 1985-86, Ministry of HRD, Department of Education, Govt. of India.

(ii) Selected Educational Statistics 1990-91, Ministry of HRD, Department of Education, Govt. of India, 1992.

The Table 4.8 also reflects that though from 1975-76 to 1995-96 the percentage of women teachers rose gradually it is still conspicuously low at all stages of education, being around 22 per cent in 1995-96. At all stages of school education the percentage of trained teachers has however been lower than the national figures and during the period of 1975-76 to 1995-96 the percentages fell from 52 to 33 in the case of middle schools, from 61 to 44 in case of primary schools and from 54 to 51 in case of secondary schools from 1980-81 to 1995-96. But one exception is shown in case of higher secondary schools whose percentages have increased from 60 to 66 over the period from 1975-76 to 1995-96. For improvement of quality of education at school level, it is imperative to have trained teachers and in order to increase enrolment of girls the percentage of women teachers also has to be raised.

Table 4.8: Teachers, Trained Teachers and Women Teachers in Institutions by Stages: 1975-76 to 1995-96

Institution	*Year*				
	1975-76	*1980-81*	*1985-86*	*1990-91*	*1995-96*
I. No. of Teachers					
Higher Secondary	310	316	587	1223	1531
Secondary	*	431	724	950	1252
Middle	424	809	1024	1671	2077
Primary	861	1438	1781	2366	2557
Total	**1595**	**2294**	**4116**	**6210**	**7417**
II. Percentage of Trained Teachers to Total					
Higher Secondary	60%	60%	52%	53%	66%
Secondary	*	54%	49%	41%	51%
Middle	52%	45%	41%	36%	33%
Primary	61%	45%	47%	35%	44%
III. Percentage of Woman Teachers to Total					
Higher Secondary	11%	13%	14%	15%	19%
Secondary	*	13%	21%	21%	23%
Middle	10%	13%	15%	19%	22%
Primary	8%	12%	17%	20%	25%

* included in Higher Secondary.

Sources: (i) Education in India, Vol. I, 1975-76, 1980-81 and 1985-86, Ministry of HRD, Department of Education, Govt. of India.
(ii) selected Educational Statistics, 1990-91, Ministry of HRD, Department of Education, Govt. of India, 1992.
(iii) Teacher Education in Arunachal Pradesh, NCTE, New Delhi, 1998.

In Arunachal Pradesh, majority of the population lives in rural areas. Though the state has tried to provide educational facilities for its people over the years a lot is still to be done to reach the all India average.

A Brief History of the Education Department

Arunachal Pradesh follows the system of single line administration with the Secretariat at the top. The role of the Secretariat is that of coordination. Below it is the Directorate of Education, which plays a pivotal role in all academic and administrative matters pertaining to education. To take care of planning and management at the districts, there are educational inspectors. The local bodies too play an important role though indirectly, in the administration of education in the State.

Educational activities were first introduced in the territory in 1947 by creating an education wing in the administration. It was headed by an Education Officer who was directly responsible to the adviser of the Governor of Assam. To make educational administration comfortable, the Assam pattern was followed in all respects by totally accepting the Assam Education Manual and even the curriculum. Partially, educational activities remained restricted to the foot hills bordering the plains of Assam and the spread of education was slow because the tribals were quite ignorant of its benefits.

After Independence as all kinds of developmental activities got momentum and people started taking interest in them there was considerable expansion in the field of education and improvement in educational administration. In 1956 the post of Education Officer was upgraded to 'Director of Education', to look after all matters related to education. The administration took care to maintain educational standards and laid special emphasis on the screening and recruitment of staff to man the new institutions and on training of staff by sending them to attend 'BT' course at Bhubaneswar and Senior/Junior Basic College at Changlang in the State.

Adequate arrangements were made for the supervision of educational activities under an Inspector of Schools assisted by Sub-Inspectors. Officers at the Directorate too helped in inspection of schools in the interior regions. Individual schools were also guided through letters and directives from the headquarters in order to safeguard the standard of education from deterioration due to rapid expansion.

In the late 70's the region known as NEFA, acquired a distinct identity of its own as a Union Territory of India and Education started growing rapidly. Then in the 80's, with the coming of the National Education Policy (NEP) and the statehood of Arunachal Pradesh, the progress became even more rapid and in order to keep up this pace of progress certain changes were incorporated in the administrative set up.

National Policy on Education

Since Arunachal Pradesh did not have its own policy statement on education, it adopted the goals and objectives of education stipulated in the National Policies of Education of 1968 and 1986. Keeping in view the recommendations of the NPE (as revised in 1992) the major aims and objectives of education in the state are:

- To remove backwardness and imbalances of the area;
- To raise the socio-economic level of the people;
- To promote national integration;
- To eradicate illiteracy;
- To universalise elementary education; and
- To acquaint the people with modern science, technology, medicine and engineering.

Since the region of the state was earlier part of Assam and was inhabited by numerous tribes with their own dialects, it had Assamese as the medium of instruction in the past; but with the adoption of the curriculum of CBSE,

English became the medium of instruction with Hindi as second language and Sanskrit/Assamese as third language to cater to the needs of the Three Language Formula.

The state chalked out its priority areas and programmes like:

– Universalisation of elementary education;

– Eradication of illiteracy; and

– Promotion of Education of girls.

Since recommendations of the NEP (1986) have had an impact on the States education system, some of its major recommendations being implemented are :

– Introduction of the new curriculum;

– Upgradation of the Teachers Training Institute at Changlang to the District Institute of Education and Training (DIET);

– Implementation of the 'Operation Blackboard' scheme;

– Adoption of measures to reform the examination system;

– Vocationalisation of education at the +2 stage;

– Introduction of pre-vocational courses at the secondary stages;

– Orientation programme for teaching and supervisory staff with regard to the introduction of the new curriculum;

– Improvement of the teaching of Science and Mathematics.

To implement these programmes and to chalk out future programmes for educational progress and achievements various commissions and committees comprising important officers and educationists were constituted by the state government in the recent past. They are as follow:

1. For identification of dialects in the different districts with the intention of teaching them in schools, a committee was constituted under the leadership of the JDPI (Academics) in 1988. It identified about 20 dialects ad suggested establishment of Education under the charge of a Joint Director of Public Instruction (JDPI).

2. To consider and facilitate the establishment of a 'State Institute of English' and to suggest a suitable location for it, an adhoc committee was constituted in 1988 under the chairmanship of the DPI which consisted of high level officers from the state as well as from other states. English being the medium of instruction in the state it approved the proposal of establishing a State Institute of English and made the following suggestions:

   (i) starting an one year correspondence-cum-contact course in "Teaching English for Academic Purposes" for teachers of all levels and subjects leading to the award of a certificate.

   (ii) Constituting the proposed course with components like:

      (a) Core English Grammar,

      (b) Spoken English

      (c) English for Social Sciences, and

      (d) English for Natural Sciences.

   (iii) Initiating a two semester residential diploma course in teaching English to proper teachers specialising in teaching of the language and for teaching at the State Institute of English; and

   (iv) Providing adequate infrastructural facilities.

In 1990, the Educational Consultants India Limited constituted a committee under the chairmanship of Prof. M.M. Kapoor of the National Institute of Educational Planning and Administration (NIEPA) for developing a 20 year perspective plan for Education in Arunachal Pradesh which comprised experts from different educational sectors, and included among others, Shri Y.D. Sharma of the UGC, Dr. J.C. Goyal and Dr. N.K. Ambusht—both from the NCERT.

A 'Task Force' for educational administration in the State was constituted in 1992 under the chairmanship of Prof. Y.N. Chaturvedi, Additional Secretary, Ministry of HRD with the distinguished officers from the reputed Institutions of India and with Shri G.C. Yadav, DPI, Arunachal Pradesh as Member Secretary.

The suggestions and recommendations of the NPE the state government also launched certain policies and prgrammes.

Elementary Education

Article 45 of the Indian Constitution enjoins on the state to provide free, compulsory and universal education to all children upto the age of 14 years, with special provision for backward and deprived groups. The state government gives it priority to provide primary education to children of age group 6-11 years through primary schools and inter-villages schools. There are also pre-primary educational centres to prepare the base for primary education. Hence, these three types of institutions cater to the diverse educational needs of the primary school children in the state. For children at elementary schools, the government has schemes like :

- Free school uniform, text books and stationery;
- Mid-day meal under nutrition programme;

- Learning through useful activities; and
- Improving the quality of education and maintaining sufficient essential facilities like posting at least 2 teachers in each primary school, constructing 2 class rooms against RLEGP fund, providing games and sports materials and play grounds, organising school games, teachers training and constituting village education committees.

Although villages located in easily accessible areas and the large and medium villages were covered by primary education during the early phase of educational programmes the small villages with population below 100 were not so fortunate. The number of such villages in the state which do not have any educational institution is 1630 (Kapoor, Vadhera and Mazumdar: 41).

Problems seem to be innumerable at the primary level of education. Participation of girls is low and many schools do not have any 'Kuchcha or Pucca' building facilities. The small villages are scattered. Their problems yet multiplied due to the rugged topography, lacking of educated villagers and their lack of interest in the education of their children. In the absence of essential facilities, the teachers also hesitate to go to small villages after posting. The number of voluntary organisation to run schools in such villages is also negligible.

Despite problems obstructing the scheme of UEE in the state, the universalisation of primary education got special attention of the government during the Eighth Five Year Plan in which the target of enrolment of children at primary stage was considerably high, i.e. from 1,18,000 to 1,45,000. It is worth mentioning that during the 1995-96 the enrolment of primary children reached about the targeted figure, i.e. 1,41,904. Even the teacher-pupil ratios as targeted finished well, i.e. 1:34 against 1:30 at the primary level and 1:20 against 1:20 at the middle school level.

Moreover, free supply of text books, uniform, stationery and clothing to tribal students were continued. Stipned was given to all rural area tribal students of class I-V to reduce drop out and enhance retention of children for UEE.

Secondary Education

In 1990-91 at the secondary stage, the percentage of girl students was 35, and at the higher secondary stage, it was only 26 per cent. The teacher pupil ratio was 1:24 in secondary and 1:21 in higher secondary schools which were far below the national averages of teacher-pupil ratio of 1:32 and 1:31 respectively. The quality of education at these two crucial levels needs considerable improvement, because for many students, these are the terminal stages of their education. Pre-vocational courses like carpentry, agriculture, horticulture, carpet weaving, knitting, painting, mechanical drawing, stenography and typing have been introduced in some secondary schools as optional subjects. Factors like lack of competent teachers in these subjects, proper facilities in the schools and motivation of the students as well as teachers have, however been responsible for its poor success.

The government has also taken initiative to improve the teaching of Science and Mathematics with financial assistance of the central government and with special reference to improving laboratory facilities in schools. Most of the schools offering science do not have a laboratory. Science laboratories with proper equipment are being provided in such schools and the existing ones are being improved by enriching them with necessary equipment. Although minimum norms of requirement for providing physical facilities in schools have to be adhered to, generally schools are opened and even upgraded at time, without adhering to the norms. Steps need to be taken to curb this practice.

State Level Setup

At present at the helm of state education affairs is the Minister of Education supported by a Deputy Minister who looks after Education. Below him is the Secretary for Education, whose secretariat exercises the powers delegated to it by the state government. Its functions include (a) looking after policy matters related to education; (b) overall supervision of education; (c) financial matters specially placed by the state government under the charge of the secretary etc. Though the Secretariat deals with policy matters, decisions are ultimately taken by the cabinet, which is accountable to the Legislature. Below the Secretary, there is the Director of Public Instruction who is assisted by four Joint Directors, three Deputy Directors, an Accounts Officer and an Administrative Officer.

Selection and Recruitment

According to a set of recruitment rules, different categories of personnel are recruited almost every year by the government. Some cases of promotion are also considered on the basis of merit and seniority, whenever the need arises. All staff in the government institutions is governed by the Central Civil Service Conduct Rules. In the state there is no State Education Service; all officers in the Department of Education belong to a common cadre under the department.

The essential requirements for appointment to the post of DPI are a second class Master's Degree with a Degree or Diploma in teaching, a minimum of 15 years of experience in the field of education and 7 years in any administrative capacity plus a minimum of 7 years regular service in any feeder post. An officer to this post is selected on the basis of merit-cum-seniority from amongst the Joint Directors/ Principal of state Institute of Education of Principals of Government Degree Colleges. In case of deputation or transfer, an IAS officer i the senior scale or an APCS officer with not less than 7 years service in selection grade in posted to this office.

The Joint Director is also expected to possess the same qualifications as the DPI. He is normally promoted to the post of DPI and the Deputy Directors to the Joint Director. In the absence of suitable candidates for promotion, the government may depute one from amongst APCS selection grade officers, though this has not been done as yet. For special posts like Deputy Directors of Public Instruction at the Directorate level, there are 13 deputy Directors of Public Instruction, newly designated as Deputy Directors of School Education (DDSE) at the district level. They are assisted by the District Adult Education Officer (DAEO), Assistant District Education Officers (ADEO) and Adult Education Supervisors (AES) for various educational activities in the district. The posts of Assistant Directors of Public Instruction/Assistant Principal are filled up solely by promotion, from the cadre of headmaster/principal.

The post of the DAEO is generally filled up by promoting an Arunachal candidate possessing qualification and experience laid down in the rules. Teachers possessing Bachelor's Degree with BT/B.Ed., and 3 years of continuous service in the grade are eligible to be appointed as ADEO/AES, on the basis of 50 percent by promotion from Junior Teachers and 50 percent by direct recruitment, subject to seniority cum-merit.

Selection and Recruitment of Teachers

Recruitment of school teachers is made by the DPI, newly designated as the Director of School Education (DSE) through advertisement and on the recommendations of duly constituted selection board. The shot-listed candidates called for interview have to take a written test in English, class room teaching of the subject and viva-voce. Candidates capable of teaching through the medium of English and willing to serve in the interior of Arunachal Pradesh are asked to apply.

Posts are reserved for SC and ST candidates as per government norms. Arunachali tribal candidates who have passed class X are selected as Assistant Teachers (Group 'B') and sent for a training of one year at the Buniadi Siksha Bhawan, Changlang. After successful completion of the training, he is absorbed as Assistant Teacher (Group 'A'). Arunachali tribal candidates who have passed class XII are eligible for the post of Assistant Teacher (Group 'A'), whereas in case of non-Arunachalis, graduation is the minimum qualification required for the post. Similarly, whereas Arunachali graduates are eligible for the post of Junior Teachers, non-Arunachalis are required to be trained graduates or second class Master's Degree holders. Arunachali candidates in adequate numbers come forward for the post of Assistant and Junior Teachers in Humanities, but very few Science graduates, specially in PCM groups, are found amongst the Arunachali candidates. The post of science teachers are normally filled up by recruiting candidates from outside the state.

Posting and Transfer

The policy of posting and transfer was formulated with a view to restricting inter-district transfer of all categories of teachers, ensuring qualitative improvement of teaching and effective supervision of schools. In very exceptional cases, inter-district transfer of teachers is considered by the DSE, although isolated cases of transfer within the district are done by the District Education Authority, with the approval of the Deputy Commissioner. To make posting and transfer of teachers easy and less complicated a method has been devised by dividing the state into three belts and posting teachers to these belts according to a set pattern. These belts are:

1. Easy Belt- Comprising schools located in the districts/subdivisional/headquarters and at places connected by motorable roads;

2. Middle Belt- Comprising schools located at places requiring walking upto five stages; and

3. Remote Belt- Comprising schools located at places requiring walking beyond five stages.

According to this policy, a teacher is not normally posted for more than two years in the easy belt, five years in the middle belt and three years in the remote belt. Each education officer maintains a register containing complete history-sheet of all categories of teachers posted in the district. The transfer/posting proposal is prepared by the district education authority according to prescribed procedure and guidelines. It is then examined by members of the District Assessment Board and submitted with their recommendations to the DSE every year in April/May. After obtaining the approval of the DSE, transfer orders of teachers as recommended by the District Assessment Board are issued.

Given the peculiar topographical conditions and communication difficulties in the state, the newly selected/recruited teachers are normally posted to schools in easily accessible areas in the easy belt at least for a year or so. It helps them adjust to the new situation. There is not special provision for consideration for posting of SC and ST teachers. However, special consideration is made for women and handicapped teachers and they are usually posted to schools in the well-connected areas. Female married teachers are generally posted at their husbands' stations of posting. This sort of special consideration sometimes badly affects the proper deployment of teachers as schools located at headquarters and in easy belts are generally found to have excess of teachers at the cost of schools located in remote areas and difficult belts, which at items experience an acute shortage of proper staff. Leave substitute teachers are appointed in the place of those deputed for training of along duration and after training they are posted back to their respective districts. Leave substitute teachers are usually absorbed against regular vacancies subject to their selection by the Board after completing all formalities. There is no provision for the appointment of part-time teachers.

As a part of the Survey, a case study was conducted in the state on the problem of 'Transfer and Posting of Teachers' (Kapoor, Vadhera and Mazumdar: 88) which explained that the Education Departments policy on transfer and posting of teachers is comprehensive as it takes into account all the related vital issues. It was also reported that there is no provision for reviewing functions of the District Assessment Boards or their recommendations. Such reviews as revealed, were to serve as desirable checks and balances on the working of the District Boards. Norms for transfer/posting of teachers are framed by the government and are generally followed and implemented fully except on very special grounds. No committee/ group has even been constituted by the state to study this problem.

Pay Scales and Service Conditions of Teachers

Teachers in the state, irrespective of whether they are employees of government schools or schools under private management have the same pay scales, qualifications and experience essential for appointment as teachers. This brings uniformity in the service conditions of all teachers working in the state. Details of qualifications and pay scales are given in Table 4.9.

Pay scales and essential qualifications in case of non-teaching staff are at par with other non-professional staff working in government institutions of the state. They are appointed by a selection board under the chairmanship of the district Deputy Commissioner DSE, and are posted on the basis of actual requirement.

Table 4.9: Pay Scale and Other Service Conditions of Teachers

Sl. No.	*Designation of Post*	*Classification*	*Qualtification & Experience Prescribed and Method of Recruitment*	*In Rs. Payscale (Revised)*
1.	Principal, H.S. School	Group 'A' Gazetted	Selection post 100% by promotion from ADSE/DEO/ Principal, BSB having at least 5 years experience.	10,000-325-15,200
2.	Headmaster Secondary School/Vice Principal H.S. School	Group 'B' Gazetted	Non selection post 100% by promotion, 75% by promotion from Junior Teacher/ Asstt. Headmaster/ Lecturer, BSB and Senior Teachers on the basis of seniority-cum-merit in the cadre of Junior Teacher. 25% from direct recruitment of Senior Teachers on seniority-cum-merit in cadre of ST subject to fulfillment of laid down conditions. In case, suitable candidates not available 25% vacancies to be diverted to eligible JT/ST on seniority-cum-merit.	8,000-275-13,500
3.	Senior Teacher (PGT) Senior Scale	Group 'C' Non-Gazetted	After completion of 8 years of service in the entry scale.	8,000-275-13,500
4.	Senior Teacher (PGT)	Group 'C' Non-Gazetted	**1. Essential:** Second Class Masters Degree in the subject concerned with Diploma/Degree in Humanities. Second Class Master's Degree in concerned subject. Preference given to those having Degree/Diploma in Education.	6,500-200-10,500

(Contd.)

Sl. No.	*Designation of Post*	*Classification*	*Qualtification & Experience Prescribed and Method of Recruitment*	*In Rs. Payscale (Revised)*
			2. Desirable: 3 years teaching experience in higher secondary school. **3.** 50% from JT on promotion; 50% direct recruitment through interview.	
5.	Junior Teacher (TGT)	Group 'C' Non-Gazetted	After completion of 8 years of service in the entry scale.	6,500-200-10,500
6.	Junior Teacher (TGT)	Group 'C' Non-Gazetted	**1. Essential:** Should have appeared and passed the subject applied for as an Elective Subject and BT/BEd. or equivalent diploma. **2. Desirable:** Post Graduate Degree in the subject applied for and 3 years teaching experience in a recognized school. **3.** Graduate for Arunachal Pradesh tribals; only 4.5% from Asstt. Teacher (A) on promotion & 50% direct recruitment through interview.	5,000-175-9,000
7.	Physical Training Instructor	Group 'C' Non-Gazetted	Hr. Sec./PUSC with certificate/diploma in Physical Education.	5,000-150-8,000
8	Lab Assistant	Group 'C' Non-Gazetted	Hr. Sec./Intermediate with Science.	4,500-125-7,000

(Contd.)

Sl. No.	Designation of Post	Classification	Qualtification & Experience Prescribed and Method of Recruitment	In Rs. Payscale (Revised)
9.	Junior Librarian	-do-	Diploma in Library Science with experience	4,500-125-7,000
10.	Asstt. Teacher (A) Selection Grade	-do-	After completion of 8 years of service in Senior Scale and recommendation from the Departmental Promotion Committee (DPC).	5,500-175-9,000
11.	Asstt. Teacher (A) Senior Scale	-do-	After the completion of 8 years of service in the entry scale.	5,000-150-8,000
12.	Asstt. Teacher (A)	-do-	**1. Essential:** For Arunachali candidate class XII and for Non-Arunachali candidate BA/BSc. **2. Desirable:** 3 year teaching experience in primary/middle school. **3.** 30% by promotion from amongst Asstt. Teachers Grade 'B', 20% from Lab Asstt. on the basis of seniority-cum-merit.	4,500-125-7,000

Source: Directorate of School Education, Establishment Branch, Arunachal Pradesh, Naharlagun.

Educational Planning

To look after the educational planning of the state, the oraganisational setup consists of a planning cell at the directorate level which is headed by the JDPI and comprises statistical personnel and office staff. At the district level, the district head of the Education Department, DDSE is incharge of educational planning. As there is no planning cell at the district level, district heads get information and data from their subordinates posted at subdivision, circle and institutional levels.

Educational planning in the state is decentralised to some extent and planning exercises are carried out at different levels, with the plan proposals being initiated at the grass-root level. At the initial stage, the plans are formulated by the local bodies, i.e. the gram panchayats at the village level. These are then scrutinised by the anchal samitees and sent to the zilla parishads and revised under the supervision and guidance of the DDSE, to be incorporated in respective district plans. The final incorporation is done by the state planning Board in accordance with guidelines received from the Centre, that is the Planning Commission and also on the basis of available financial and other resources.

Thus, in the State, the system of educational planning involves the three tiers of the Panchayat Raj system educational administrators at the district and state level; the Planning Cell of the Directorate of Public Instruction; the Secretary of Education, the Department of Planning and Department and the State Planning Board.

No modern techniques of educational planning are used in the state; only simple compilation of data is resorted to. There is no organisational provision to apply corrective measures, if needed at the mid-state of implementation of plans and programmes. Adhoc arrangements are made in the case such measure becomes indispensable.

School Text Books

All the secondary and higher secondary schools managed by the government as well as these with non-government managements, follow the CBSE syllabi and course. Text books published by NCERT, CBSE and also by other publishers recommended by CBSE are followed. At the elementary level of education, usually NCERT books are followed. However to cater to the needs and aspiration of the child and to maintain and acquaint him with the social and cultural aspects, a few text books like New Dawn Reader, Part I, II and III in English, Arun Bharati, Part I, II and III in Hindi and Social Studies for class III have been prepared specially by the NCERT for children attending primary classes in Arunachal Pradesh.

All the text books are produced by the Directorate of School Education on the basis of the requirements submitted by the DDSEs of the districts. A consolidated list of the requirement of text books in the state level is prepared and then forwarded to the government for its sanction. Most of the books are procured from NCERT, and an advance payment alongwith demand list of requirement of text books to be despatched directly to the DDSE of the concerned district, is sent to the council well ahead of the academic session so that text books can be made available to the students at the beginning of the session. In case of books to be procured from other publishers, the same procedure is followed; the only difference being that payment is made after receiving the books. As soon as books are received by the DDSEs from the concerned publishers, the DSE is informed about payment. Generally, schools located in towns and nearby areas collect the text books from the DDSE on receipt of information about their arrival. In case of interior schools, books are despatched through ADEO/AES and such officers responsible for the educational activities of the block.

Free text books are supplied to the Arunachali tribal students upto the middle school level. For secondary and higher secondary stages, students have to bear 25% of the cost of books. Non-Arunachali students have to bear the full price. Sale amounts of the text books are deposited in the treasury. Each school is expected to maintain necessary prescribed records and registers which are generally shown to the inspecting Officer of the Directorate at the time of inspection.

Inspite of sincere efforts made to ensure timely procurement and distribution of text books some consignments of text books especially from NCERT and CBSE are received quite late. Sometimes due to certain reasons beyond their control, books are received after many months or even at the end of the session. This causes serious set-back to the timely completion of the prescribed course in schools and also leads to various complaints from students, teaching staff and public. Some arrangement should therefore be made by the NCERT and CBSE to remove this bottleneck and ensure the despatch of books at the proper time before the commencement of the academic session in the state.

Curriculum, Courses and Syllabi

A national curriculum for elementary and secondary education has been prepared by the NCERT. This has been implemented in all the schools of the State on the basis of recommendations of the Central Board of Secondary Education (CBSE) and in a phased manner as shown below:

1988-89–Textual materials developed by NCERT for classes I, II and IV were introduced.

1989-90–Text books developed by NCERT and CBSE according to revised curriculum for classes II, IV, VII, IX and XI were prescribed.

1990-91—As per the NCERT and CBSE guidelines, revised curriculum was implemented in classes V, VIII, X and XII.

The pre-primary education of two years duration is provided for children belonging to the age group 4 to 5+. At this stage no formal teaching of subjects is undertaken. To make the learning experience a joyous one, play way techniques, group activities and games are adopted to keep pre-school children busy for three hours a day.

The elementary education comprises primary classes I to V and upper primary (middle) classes VI to VIII. A primary school generally functions for five hours a day, out of which, four hours are spent on teaching. Value education and co-curricular activities occupy an important place. The subjects taught at the primary level are English, Hindi, Mathematics, Environmental Studies, work experience and Health/Physical Education and Value Education. At the Upper primary level, subject like : English, Hindi 3rd Language, Mathematics Science, Social Science, Work Experience, Art Education, and Health/Physical Education and value Education are taught.

The secondary education consists of classes IX and X and the duration of the school is six hours a day out of which five hours are spent on teaching and one hour on morning assembly and recess. The Curriculum taught includes, English (Course A), Hindi (Course B), 3rd Language (Sanskrit), Mathematics, Science, Social Science (History and Geography Classes IX and X), Economics (class IX only) and Civics (Class X only), work experience, Art Education, Health and Physical Education, Value Education.

The higher secondary stage consists of classes XI and XII where a student opts out according to his ability and performance, any one of the three steams, i.e., Science, Humanities and Commerce. The subjects taught in different streams fall under two broad groups—Core and Elective.

For all streams, there are elective subjects which a student chooses. The common curriculum for all is English (Core), General Studies, Work Experience, Health/Physical Education and Value Education.

The state government has already decided to introduce Sanskrit as 3rd Language in the schools in a phased manner. Accordingly, it was introduced in class VI in 1990-91. Prior to that, Assamese/Sanskrit was the 3rd Language. The government has also decided to develop the local dialects and prepare graded books for introduction as 3rd Language in a phased manner from 1992-93. Twenty major dialects have so far been identified for development of learning materials. A separate wing regarding text book production has been opened (Kapoor, Vadhera and Mazumdar: 131).

Students' Evaluation

To bring about an improved quality of education, the system of continues evaluation has been adopted by schools at different educational levels. Since secondary and higher secondary schools have been affiliated to the CBSE, students have to appear in the AISSE for class X and AISSCE for class XII. The Directorate conducts examinations only for the students of class V, VIII, IX and XI. Respective schools conduct examinations for classes I to IV, VI and VII.

The weightage of periodic tests/assignments etc. in respect of classes I to IX and XI are as follows :

(i)	Unit Test	–	10%
(ii)	Assignment/Home work	–	10%
(iii)	Half yearly examination	–	20%
(iv)	Annual examination	–	60%

A student has to secure 35% marks in total in each subject and 25% marks in the external/annual examinations. In case of 3rd Language, SUPW/Work Experience, tests are conducted internally by the concerned school before commencement of the external examination and grades on a 7 point scale are awarded.

Smooth conducting of primary, middle, secondary and higher secondary examinations becomes the duty of the two district organising committees; Committee for Primary and Middle Examination consisting of (i) DDSE as the chairman, (ii) Principal of H.S. School (iii) Headmaster of Secondary School (iv) Teacher-in-charge of Primary School and (v) Headmaster of Middle School all as Members and Committee for Secondary and Higher Secondary School Examination comprising (i) Deputy Commissioner as chairman, (ii) Principal of H.S. School as vice-chairman, (iii) DDSE as Member Secretary and (iv) Headmaster of Secondary School as Member.

These committees have the responsibility to fix examination centres, appointment the centre superintendent, get examinees' answer scripts evaluated and compile, finalise and declare the results. Question papers and answer scripts are supplied to the DDSE of the concerned districts by the Directorate before commencement of the examinations. They are further supplied to the Principal, H.S. School acting as the vice-chairman of the organising Committee. Centre charges are admissible to each centre for procuring necessary examination materials. The examiners get the remuneration for evaluating the answer scripts. According to government norms TA/DA is paid to the centre superintendents and invigilators.

In case of secondary and higher secondary examinations, students who fail in one subject, have to sit for a compartmental examination. Compartmental examination is conducted by the concerned Principal/Headmaster in the month of July, at the beginning of the new session. For class IX and XI examinations, examination fees are collected from the students. Examination fee alongwith a list of candidates is sent to the Directorate by the concerned DDSE/Principals well in advance. Setting of question papers, moderation and printing are arranged by the Directorate.

Inspection and Supervision

Inspection and supervision of institutions to play a key role in the educational administration to help improve the state of school education. At the district level the DDSEs are incharge of the inspection and supervision of all schools upto higher secondary level. They are assisted in this respect by the ADEOs and AES, who generally look after the inspection and supervision of all primary and middle schools in the specific block under them. Under these officers, there is a Statistical Assistant and the Office staff. The ADEO/AES reports to this DDSE in connection with their findings and suggestions.

The DDSE conducts panel inspection of secondary and higher secondary schools. The headmasters of various schools and relevant subject specialists drawn from higher secondary schools alongwith the Deputy Director comprise the panel. During the inspection of a school, emphasis on investigating whether the physical and financial targets have been achieved or not. Teaching in general or quality of teaching a specific subject depend on factors like enrolment of students, strength of staff, examination results of the last three years, achievement of schedule of work, difficulties encountered by the school etc. In reality due to shortage of time at the disposal of the inspecting officers, most of the forms are returned blank. Consequently, the authority fails to take up follow up actions on the basis of reports. Hence, the very purpose of inspection and supervision of schools gets hampered.

In a calendar year, one educational institution is expected to be inspected twice, once at the beginning of the year and other at the end. For inspecting a primary school, a day is enough, for a middle school at lest two days and three days for a secondary or higher secondary school. It is beyond expectation to maintain the frequency of inspecting a school twice a year, particularly in the schools located in the remote and interior areas of the state. Other factors affecting such frequency are the shortage of inspecting officers and lack of proper transport facilities for these officers.

Since all officers at the inspectorate are always under heavy pressure of work, the need for modernising the inspection and supervision process is actually felt.

Future Perspectives

According to the Sixth All India Educational Survey there are 3834 habitations in Arunahcal Pradesh out of which 2030 habitations do not have primary education facilities within a distance of 1 km. Out of these 2030 habitations 1968 have population between 100-299 and the rest 62 have population of 300 and above (NCTE 1998: 67). Therefore, mostly small habitations are yet to be covered up by providing primary education facilities. Since most of these habitations have population below 200, it is feasible to provide primary schools in such small habitations. Alternative arrangements are to be made for all such locations to facilitate the children living in these areas to get primary education.

The girls participation at the Primary and Middle stages has been achieved to the extent of 44.48% and 42.45% respectively. Their participation in primary education is much less than the boys due to their engagement in domestic work. Serious thought has been given for increasing their participation in primary education for achieving the objectives of UEE and since new measures are now being thought of for attracting more girls to schools, They are :

(i) Special scholarship to girls (belonging to poor families) of the state from classes I-VIII. Those girls who are not getting stipend in lieu of ration will get this benefit.

(ii) Providing girls' hostel in every Middle and Inter-village Primay School.

(iii) Providing better physical facilities in all the schools for attracting more girls.

(iv) Construction of residential quarters for posting more lady teachers to the schools for taking special care of girls and increasing their enrolment.

The above steps may be helpful to check the dropout rate of girl which is at present 65% against 55% for that of boys at the primary stage. The dropout rate is a great barrier for UEE and therefore, special steps are to be taken for their retention in the schools for UEE.

To launch the above mentioned special schemes and to see their proper implementation and to provide infrastructural facilities to the schools the government needs huge funds since the cost of construction in the difficult areas of the state due to lack of transport and communication facilities is quite high. Communication is a point for which the government is unable to send lady teachers to difficult locations to take care of girls' education. In the state most of teachers are from the different states of the country and it is the governments' responsibility to provide accommodation to all of them since the provision for teachers' residential quarters is a very important component in the state's educational setup.

For qualitative improvement of primary education the Government of India has launched the scheme of Operation Blackboard. Arunachal Pradesh also avails the benefit of the centrally sponsored scheme. The central Government has been helping the state under the scheme by providing the cost of teaching-learning equipment and salary of the second teacher in primary schools and construction of the school buildings under the scheme is the state's responsibility. The government has so far covered 952 primary schools under the scheme and posted 526 teachers to convert single teacher primary schools to double teacher schools. The state is now getting the benefit of Central grants under Operation Blackboard for strengthening the middle schools by providing teaching-learning equipment.

For qualitative improvement of teacher one DIET has been established at Changlang for training of teachers. Moreover, the Government of India has also released Rs. 500 lakhs for establishment of 10 DIETs in 10 districts of the state. This grant is 50% of the requirement for construction of buildings (NCTE 1998: 69). Some of the effective steps have been taken for construction of buildings within this grant during the financial year 1997-98. Steps are also being taken to make all the DIETs functional by completing minimum basic physical facilities as well as overcoming the difficulties that the state has been facing in recruitment of fully qualified instructors for the DIETs.

Expansion of School Education During the 9th Plan

Primary Schools

It is proposed to establish 100 primary schools during the 1st year of the 9th plan for coverage of all those habitations having population above 200 which do not have primary education facilities within a walking distance of 1 km. These are 453 uncovered habitations in the population slab of 100-299 out of which 38 habitations in the population slab of 200-299 are proposed to be covered up by providing a primary school and the remaining 415 habitations in the population slab of 100-199 may also be covered by providing community schools during the 1st year of the plan. As regards uncovered habitations below 100 population slab, it is proposed to cover them by bringing these children to the I.V. primary schools having facilities.

In connection with the establishment of 100 primary schools during the first year of the 9th Plan, it is worth mentioning that two teachers (1JT + 1AT) will be provided in the first year of establishment and a third (AT) may be provided in the third year. All the primary schools will have one year pre-primary class and classes I-V. Under the norms of the Operation Blackboard (OB) two teachers are supposed to be there in a primary school of classes I-V. But since one additional pre-primary class is proposed, provision is their for a third teacher. In the 4th year, it is proposed to provide 4th teacher (AT) as the enrolment is expected to exceed 100 in classes I-V for which 3 teachers are required as per OB norms and 1 additional teacher for pre-primary. Financial implications for establishing new primary schools are shown in Table 4.10.

Table 4.10: Financial Implications for Opening New Primary Schools

Plan year	*Recurring*		*Non-recurring*		*Total*
	Salaries	*Equipment & Textbooks*	*School & Teacher Quarters*	*Furniture*	
1997-98	66.00	30.00	1000.00	30.00	1126.00
1998-99	132.00	10.00	–	20.00	162.00
1999-2000	162.00	15.00	–	20.00	197.00
2000-01	222.00	20.00	250.00	20.00	512.00
2001-02	260.00	25.00	–	20.00	305.00
Total	842.00	100.00	1250.00	110.00	2302.00

Source: Plan Proposals (9th Plan) and Publications of Government of Arunachal Pradesh.

Primary Teachers

Around 187 Inter-village residential schools are there in the state at present where the children from uncovered habitations are to study in the hostels and get education from pre-primary to class V. It is expected that around 200 children will get education in each of the I-V primary school for which proper facilities are required to be provided. For classes I-V and pre-primary, a minimum of 7 teachers are required to be provided in each school. Out of these existing primary schools, it is required to convert another 13 primary schools into I-V schools. Thus (187 + 13)=200 I-V schools will function in the state asking their teachers strength to be 200 x 7 = 1400 during the 9th plan.

Since 1100 primary schools including 200 I-V will function in the state there will be 900 primary schools of non-residential type which are to be provided with one teacher for pre-primary class and 3 teachers for classes I-V, hence asking the teachers strength to be 900 x 4 = 3600. In addition to these primary schools there will be another 550 primary sections in 550 middle schools in which 4 teachers are to be there, hence once again demanding a teachers' strength of 550 x 4 = 2200. Altogether (1400 + 3600 + 2200) = 7200 teachers are required against the plan out of which a strength of 3748 teachers exists now at the primary stage. So, an additional requirement of 3452 teachers is needed.

Out of 3452 additional teachers required at the primary stage, the state has already incorporated the financial requirement of 400 teachers in the newly proposed 100 primary schools. Thus, the financial implications for the remaining 3052 teachers are shown in Table 4.11.

Middle Schools

For coverage of all children in the age group of 11-14 years the ratio of number of primary and middle schools during the 9th plan should 2:1. Against the proposed 1100 primary schools to be functional within the plan, there should be 550 middle schools to bring their ratio to 2:1. At present there exists only 300 middle schools in the state. Hence, it is required to upgrade 250 primary schools to middle schools during the 1st year of the plan so that the state can achieve

Table 4.11: Finan‹ial Implications for Additional Primary Teachers

(Rs. in lakhs)

Plan Year	*Target No. of School*	*Salaries*	*Teacher Quarters*	*Total*
1997-98	1052	315.60	2630.00	2945.60
1998-99	1000	931.20	2500.00	3431.20
1999-2000	1000	1531.00	2500.00	4031.00
2000-01		1831.00	–	1831.00
2001-02		1840.00	–	1840.00
Total	**3052**	**6448.80**	**7630.00**	**14078.00**

UEE within the plan period. While upgrading a primary school to middle school, the government may provide two teachers in the first year (one HM + one JT), two teachers in the second year (2 JT) and one teacher in third year for teaching Science, Mathematics, Social Science and Language. Mention may be made most of the middle schools have to be provided with hostel facilities for both boys and girls so that the children of the feeder schools coming from distant places may be accommodated there for continuation of their studies at the middle level. The Table 4.12 shows the financial implications for upgradation of 250 primary schools to middle schools.

Against the proposed establishment of new schools and upgradation of schools, additional rooms are to be constructed. Existing 1200 primary schools are to be provided with one additional room for pre-primary class. Further, newly proposed 100 primary schools are also to be provided with 3 class rooms. Thus, for primary schools (1200 + 300) = 1500 class rooms are to be constructed. Regarding 250 new middle schools, 3 class rooms are to be provided for upper primary (middle) section in each school. Therefore, for 250 schools, 750 class rooms are required. Other

Table 4.12: Financial Implications for Upgrading Primary Schools to Middle Schools

(Rs. in lakhs)

Plan Year	*Salaries*	*Equipment & Textbook Stipend*	*School Teacher's Quarters*	*Furniture*	*Total*
1997-98	195.00	100.00	17625.00	125.00	18045.00
1998-99	570.00	162.50	–	100.00	832.50
1999-2000	840.00	187.50	–	100.00	1127.50
2000-01	930.00	212.50	–	100.00	1242.50
2001-02	940.00	237.50	–	100.00	1277.50
Total	**3475.00**	**900.00**	**17625.00**	**525.00**	**22525.00**

Source: Plan Proposals (9th Plan) and Publications of Government of Arunachal Pradesh.

750 class rooms are also required to be provided in the existing primary and middle schools hence altogether needing 300 class rooms to be constructed. Out of 300 class rooms financial implications of 300 class rooms for new primary and 750 for new middle schools have already been included. For the remaining 1950 classrooms the financial implications are given in Table 4.13 (Rs. 39 crores).

In addition to this, the provision for water and toilet facilities in the proposed primary (1000) and upper primary classrooms (500) is expected to incur Rs. 10 crores and Rs. 5 crores respectively, a total of Rs. 15 crores.

Middle School Teachers

The total requirement of teachers for 550 middle school is 2750 (5 teachers per school inclusive of one Headmaster). At present the existing number of teachers at the middle schools is 1224. Thus, additional (2750 – 1224) = 1526 teachers are to be provided during the 9th plan. Out of

Table 4.13: Financial Implications for Constructing Additional Class Rooms

(Rs. in lakhs)

Plan Year	*Physical Target Class Rooms*	*Total*
1997-98	700	1400.00
1998-99	700	1400.00
1999-2000	550	1100.00
2000-01	–	–
2001-02	–	–
Total	**1950**	**3900.00**

Source: Plan Proposals (9th Plan) and Publications, Government of Arunachal Pradesh.

1526 teachers the government has already incorporated 750 teachers in the proposal of upgradation of 250. Financial implications for the balance (1526 – 750) = 776 teachers during the plan are shown in Table 4.14.

Table 4.14: Financial Implications for Additional Teachers of Middle School Level

Plan Year	*Target No. of Teachers*	*Recurring Salaries*	*Non-recurring Teacher's Quarters*	*Total*
1997-98	300	108.00	750.00	858.00
1998-99	300	324.00	750.00	1074.00
1999-2000	176	495.36	440.00	935.00
2000-01	–	500.00	–	500.00
2001-02	–	525.00	–	525.00
Total	**776**	**1952.36**	**1940.00**	**3892.00**

Source: Plan Proposals (9th Plan) and Publications, Government of Arunachal Pradesh.

Provision of Text Books and Instructional Materials

At the elementary stage the present enrolment of students is about 1,80,000 against the projected child population of 1,80,000 in the age group of 6-14 years. Thus, the gross coverage in the age group 6-14 years is about 100 per cent, but due to enrolment of under-age and over-age children in classes I-VIII, the net coverage is about 80%. Therefore, another 20% of the child population are to be enrolled in the schools for 100% net coverage which means due to increase of population there will be an additional enrolment of 36,000 plus another 4,000 total coming to 40,000. The break up of number of children in the primary middle school stages year-wise for coverage of additional children under UEE is given in Table 4.15.

Table 4.15: Enrolment Target for UEE

Plan Year	*Enrolment Target*		
	Classes I-V	*Classes VI-VIII*	*Total (I-VIII)*
1997-98	5,000	5,000	10,000
1998-99	5,000	6,000	11,000
1999-2000	1,000	6,000	7,000
2000-01	1,000	5,000	6,000
2001-02	1,000	5,000	6,000
Total	**13,000**	**27,000**	**40,000**

Source: Plan Proposals (9th Plan) and Publications, Government of Arunachal Pradesh.

All these children are to be provided with text books free of cost and the newly proposed 100 primary and 250 middle schools are also to be provided teaching learning equipments (TLE) as per OB norms @ Rs. 25,000/- per primary school and Rs. 50,000/- per middle school and

10% of the amount from the subsequent year for replacement of items. The financial implications for providing teaching learning materials are shown Table 4.16.

Table 4.16: Financial Implications for Providing Teaching Learning Material

(Rs. in lakhs)

Plan Year	*Text Books*	*TLE to Primary*	*TLE to Middle*	*Total*
1997-98	30.00	25.00	125.00	180.00
1998-99	63.00	2.50	12.50	78.00
1999-2000	84.00	2.50	12.50	99.00
2000-01	103.00	2.50	12.50	118.00
2001-02	120.00	2.50	12.50	135.00
Total	**400.00**	**35.00**	**175.00**	**610.00**

Source: Plan Proposals (9th Plan) and Publications, Government of Arunachal Pradesh.

It is thus estimated that additional resources are required for different items of expenditure to the tune of Rs. 530 crores during the 9th plan.

Strengthening Teacher Education

Expansion of school education in the state to cover the need of ensured habitations and upgradation of some primary schools to middle schools will call for an adequate number of fresh trained teachers. The existing teachers will have to be suitable trained both in subject content and pedagogy. The Table 4.17 shows the position of trained and untrained teachers in the state.

The Table 4.17 indicates out of a total 8355 teachers, as many as 4896 teachers (58.6%) are untrained. The number of untrained teachers has risen by about 800 since 1995-96, a rise of 10% over a couple of years which is a matter of

Table 4.17: District-wise Break-up of Trained/ Untrained Teachers (1997-98)

District	*Trained*	*Untrained*	*Male*	*Female*	*Total*
Tawang	82	160	204	38	242
West Kameng	318	282	451	149	600
East Kameng	92	211	274	29	303
Lower Subansiri	285	246	458	73	531
Upper Subansiri	170	392	491	71	562
Papum-Pare	356	635	520	471	991
West Siang	658	527	985	200	1185
East Siang	302	713	775	240	1015
Upper Siang	96	165	239	22	261
Dibang Valley	165	286	350	101	451
Lohit	367	526	604	289	893
Changlang	234	432	528	138	666
Tirap	334	321	461	194	655
Total	**3459**	**4896**	**6340**	**2015**	**8355**

Source: Directorate of School Education Government of Arunachal Pradesh, Naharlagun.

great concern. A serious effort is to be made to ensure the backlog of untrained teachers liquidated with 9th Five Year Plan period. At the same time the Arunachal Government shall have to observe that fresh inflow of untrained teachers is not allowed. This requires a proper recruitment policy for appointment of new teachers on the one hand and adequate arrangements to ensure the supply of required number of trained teachers to the school system at the elementary as well as secondary level on the other.

Thus, in order to raise the quality of teacher education at different levels which may ultimately uplift the quality of school education in the state, it is high time that the teachers training institutes are continuously upgraded. In this context, Arunachal Pradesh shall have to joint hands with other neighbouring states. The Regional Institute of Education of the NCERT, which has been recently set up at Shillong may prove to be a necessary guide in this line. Arunachal Pradesh to arrest all sorts of bottlenecks in the sphere of school education should utilise the benefits of this advantage to the fullest possible extent.

5

THE DISTRICT: WEST KAMENG

West Kameng district of Arunachal Pradesh is lying approximately between $91^{0}30$ to $92^{0}40$ East Longitude; and $26^{0}54$ to $28^{0}01$ North Latitudes. The district is surrounded by Tibet region of China in the North, Bhutan in the West; Tawang and East Kameng districts of Arunachal Pradesh are in the North-West and East respectively. The southern boundary adjoins Sonitpur and Darrang districts of Assam.

Historical Genesis

The name of the district is derived from the Kameng river, a tributary of the Brahmaputra that flows through the district. Till 1914, the district was a part of the Darrang district of Assam. By a Government of India Notification of 1914 the are covered by this district became a part of the "Western Sector" of the 'North East Frontier Tract' to which the entry of the British subject was regulated by an 'Inner Line'. In 1919, this tract was renamed as the 'Balipara Frontier Tract' having its headquarter at Charduar of Assam. In 1946, the district area was carved out of the Balipara Frontier Tract with the name of Sela Sub-agency and its headquarters continued to be at Charduar. In 1945, Sela Sub-agency was renamed as the Kameng Frontier Division and its headquarters was later transferred to Bomdila. Like other part of the NEFA, it was also under the ministry of External Affairs and over all in charge of the district was a Political Officer. Later Kameng Frontier Division was renamed as Kameng district and the Political Officer was redesigned as Deputy Commissioner.

On 1st June 1980, Kameng district was bifurcated into East and West Kameng districts, East Kameng was formed covering the area of then Seppa Sub-division and rest of the area of the erstwhile Kameng district was placed under the West Kameng. Finally, on 6th October, 1984 West Kameng district was further bifurcated and the Tawang Sub-division became the Tawang district.

Physiography

The topography of the district is mostly mountainous, A greater part of it falls within the higher mountain zone consisting a mass of angled peaks and valleys.

In West Kameng there are three principal mountain ranges a part of Sela range, Bomdila range and Foothills range. The Sela range consists of a series of mountains arranged in form of a big line from Tibet in the North, Bhutan in the West thereby forming a tough terrain to pass through it.

The altitude of Sela range, varies from 14000′ to 15000 and Sela Pass is 13714′ high valley of river Dirangchu, a tributary of Kameng river. On this range, the district head-quarters, Bomdila lies at the altitude varying from 8100′ to 9000′ above sea level. South of the Bomdila ranges lies the Foothills range which is full of tropical forests with trees of great economic value and with various types of wild game.

The Kameng river flows through the district and leaving the district at Bahlukpong, it ultimately joins the Brahma-putra in the plain of Assam. The Tenga , Bichom and the Dirangchu are the main tributaries of the river Kameng.

Climate

The district is situated within the temperate zone and remote from sea. The sea has thus no influence on its climate and the distance from Equator in immaterial owing to influence of the snow-clad mountains. The only factor which determines the climate is the direction and height of mountain and the nature of the soil.

Although the district lies close to the tropic, it furnishes every gradation of climate from the sultry suffocating tropical heat of foothill area to the arctic cold snow clad peaks. Thus the climate is hot and humid upto 4000′ in southern area, temperate upto 7000′ and cold beyond it. Humidity is generally high throughout the year, the winter months being less humid.

Population

As per 1991 census, West Kameng District is having 170 villages with a population of 56, 421 comprising 30,966 males and 25,455 females. Bomdila town has a population of 5,655 persons. The literate population of the district as per 1991 census was 20,585 forming 36.48 percent of the total population. However, literacy among males and females was recorded as 44.72 percent and 27.06 percent respectively. The average density of population per square kilometer is 8 for the district as compared to 10 persons for Arunachal Pradesh. The district headquarters Bomdila is declared as urban and the rest of the district is consider rural. The sex ratio indicated 822 females per 1000 males. The decennial growth rate of population (1981-1991) was recorded as 35.73 for the district.

Local Inhabitants

There are five major tribes in West Kameng namely Monpas, Mijis, Akas, Sherdukpens and Khawas.

Monpa

The Monpas belong to the Tibeto - Mongoloid Stock. They are well-built, fair in complexion and medium to tall in structure. They are hospitable, gentle and unassuming in temperament. Some of them have good business acumen.

Their houses are made of stone and timber. A Monpa family is patriarchal. Monogamy is a general rule though polygamy is also practised. Mopas have castes and clans with no social hierarchy. Due to slight variation in dialects monpas can be divided into six linguistic groups, namely Tawang Monpa, Dirang Monpa, Lish Monpa, Boot Monpa, Kalaktang Monpa and Panchen Monpa. Each group has its own dialect.

Monpas are Mahayan Buddhists by religion with close cultural and religious affinities with Bhutanese and Tibetans. All houses have small altar and chapels and statue of lord Buddha. Offering water in little cups and burning butter lamps are daily rituals. They believe in the transmigration of soul and reincarnation.

The Monpas perform many pantomime out of which the "Ajilamu" dance is very popular. Losar and Choskar are the major religious festivals of the Monpas. Losar is celebrated to commemorate the advent of the new year. In choskar the Lamas read religious scriptures in the Gompa for a number of days. There after, the villagers carry the religious books on their back in the procession under the guidance of senior Lama and procession goes around the cultivation fields. The significance of this performance is to ensure better harvests and protection of grains from insects and wild animals and also for the prosperity of the villagers in general.

The Monpas are agriculturists. They practise both shifting and permanent type of cultivation. They keep horses, yaks, cows, pigs sheep and fowls. They do hunting by net, angle and trap. The Monpas are known for Wood carving, planting religious scrolls called Thankals, Carpet Making and Weaving.

Miji (Dhammai)

The Mijis in the valley of Bichom river and they are a small group of people. According to their own tradition and belief they had originally migrated from the plains and they even claim to have connections with the Ahom kings who rules over Assam (Statistical Handbooks of West Kameng District, 1997: 4). Marriage among the Mijis usually takes place by negotiation. Normally bride price is given by parents of the bridegroom.

The Mijis belong to the mongoloid stock. They are divided into two classes, the Myullu and Nyulla who do not intermarry. Their religion is indigenous but they have come under certain amount of Buddhist influence.

The Miji family is patriarchal. They put prominent tattoo marks on their faces. Basketry is a popular handicraft among the men-folk. They are agriculturists and practise shifting cultivation. They also do hunting and fishing.

The Mijis observe a number of ceremonies in the village, the most important being the phone oghin or the Chindang. They believe in many gods. Each village has a Deore or priest who officiates in the rituals.

There is a village council in each Mijis village and the council consists of village headman and other leaders of the village.

Aka (Hrusso)

The Akas live in the south-eastern part of the district. Their main concentration in noticed in the Thrizino area.

The Aka society is said to be mainly based on two main groups: Kutsun and Kavatsun. An Aka family is patriarchal and polygamy is practised. Marriage takes place either by the common way of negotiation or by elopements. Cross cousin marriage is normally preferred. Mithuns are the essential part of the bride price for marriage. The Aka house is an elongated structure. The Akas have prominent tattoo marks on the face. They observe a number of ceremonies in the village. The most important community festival is known as Nechido, performed by village priest once in a year.

The Aka women make colourful bags. Basket weaving is the popular handicraft among the men-folk. The most common form of art is wood-painting.

The Akas are agriculturists and they practice shifting cultivation. They keep mithuns, cows, horses, goats, pigs and poultry. They practise hunting and chasing by means of spears.

Sherdukpen

The Sherdukpens belong to the Tibeto-Mongoloid stock and they. are fair in complexion. Their main concentration is over four main village of Rupa, Jigaon, Shergoan and Thongree. However, at present some of them are settled in Kamengbari area of the district.

The Sherdukpen society is based on two classes, Tong and Chao. The Thongs are said to be descedant of the King Japtang. Burach and Chaos are the descendants of his partners and assistants. The Thong enjoys a traditional superiority. These two broad classes are again divide into many clans.

A Sherdukpen family is patriarchal and they practise monogamous type of marriage. Houses are generally erected on substantial stone-foundations. The floor and walls are made of thick wooden planks.

Like Monpas, the Sherdukpens are also Buddhists and deeply religious. They observe a number of ceremonies, the important ones are (a) Choskar, (b) Losar (c) Wang and (d) Khiksiwa. The Choskar, Losar and Wang are Buddhist ceremonies. Khiksiwa is a non-Buddhist ceremony and celebrated at the out-skirts of the village.

The Sherdukpens are agriculturists and practise both shifting and permanent cultivation. They keep livestock like ponies, cows, goats, sheep, fowls, and bullocks. They hunt with bows and arrows. They practise fishing by means of nets, angles and traps. The Sherdukpen women are skilled weavers. The Sherdukpens perform many dances. The principal dances are the Yak dance, and the Ajilamu dance which are both exciting and entertaining. An interesting feature of the Shedukpen life used to be their annual migration during the winter months to Doimara and in the adjoining with the plains.

Khawa (Bugun)

The Khawas inhabit in some of the villages of Thrizino circle of the District. They call themselves Buguns. The tribe is sub-divided into a number of clans. All of them are said to have originated from a single tribe identity called "Achimpimbu". The tribe endogamy and clan-exogamy is the rule of the tribe. Monogamy is the social norm, but sometimes bigamy is also practised.

A Khawa family is patriarchal The Khawas belong to the Mongoloid stock and are of fair complexion. They have flat nos, conspicuous cheek bones, black hair and brownish eyes. Both males and females keep long hairs and tie their hair like the Akas and the Mijis. The Khawa houses are like those of the Akas and Mijis but roof of the houses are usually covered with bamboo mattings. They are argiculturists. They practise shifting cultivation and keep domesticated animals like cows, horses, pigs, sheeps, goats, fowls, and very rarely mithuns. They use to hunt and chase by means of spears, traps, bows and arrows.

The most important ceremonies among them is the 'Kshyatowal'. The village priest (Phabi) performs the ritual and ceremonies. The Khawas have a number of songs and dances which are mainly associated with their socio-religious festivals.

Administrative Setup

The administrative setup is based on single line administration which aims at keeping a close cooperation amongst various developments with the administration and thus work together for speedy development of the people and the area.

The entire district is divided into three sub-divisions, viz. Bomdilla, Rupa and Thrizino. Bomdila Sub-division has two circles, i.e., Dirang and Bomdila (Sadar), Rupa Sub-division covers Kalaktang and Singchung circles, Thrizino Sub-division has got three circles namely, Nafra, Thrizino and Jameri.

As per Government notification Bhalukpong is under Thrizino sub-division for developmental purpose and under Rupa sub-division for maintaining law and order.

The Deputy Commissioner, being the overall incharge of the district, maintains law and order with the help of the administrative officers and police force. The villages have their own customary administrative officers and police force. The villages have their own customary administrative system in the form of traditional village councils. The Assam Frontier Regulation Act, 1945, authorises the village councils to settle all civil matters the Deputy Commissioner and some other administrative officers have jurisdiction under the supervision of the Assam High Court which holds the appellate and the revision authority.

The district has been covered by three blocks : Dirang, Kalaktang and Nafra-Buragaon.

The Panchayat Raj has been introduced in the district with the North East Frontier Agency Panchayat Raj Regulation, 1967. Under this regulation :

1. The Gram Panchayat exists at the village level,
2. The Anchal Samity at the Anchal level and

3. The Zilla Parisad at the district level.

The regulation provides for effective participation of the people in the administration through the institutions set up under the Panchayat Raj Scheme.

Highlights of Important Aspects of West Kameng District

1. Area	:	7422 Sq. km.
2. Administrative sub-divisions	:	3
3. Administrative Circles	:	10
4. No. of Blocks	:	3
5. No. of Towns	:	1
6. No. of Villages (as per 1991 census)	:	170
7. Total population as per 1991 census	:	56,421
(a) Male	:	30,966
(b) Female	:	24,455
8. Total Urban Population (as per 1991 census)	:	5,655
(a) Male	:	3,243
(b) Female	:	2,412
9. Total Literate Population	:	20,585
10. Percentage of Literacy	:	36.48%
(a) Male	:	44.72%
(b) Female	:	27.06%
11. Density of Population	:	8 persons per sq. km.
12. Sex Ratio (Females per 1000 males)	:	822

13. Decennial Growth Rate of Population (1981-91)	:	35.74
14. No. of Assembly Constituencies	:	4
15. Name of Indigenous STs in the district	:	a. Monpa
	:	i. Dirang Monpa
	:	ii. Lish Monpa
	:	iii. Boot Monpa
	:	iv. Kalaktang Monpa
	:	v. Panchen Monpa
	:	b. Miji
	:	c. Sherdukpen
	:	d. Aka
	:	e. Bugun (Khawa)
16. Important Rivers	:	a. Kameng (Khawa)
		b. Tenga
		c. Bichom
		d. Gochem
		e. Dirangchu
		f. Norgum (Bhairab Kund)
		g. Jamuri (Dhansiri)
17. Hydel Project with capacity	:	a Dirang (2000 KW)
		b. Rahung (750 KW)
		c. Sessa (1500 KW)
		d. Rupa (200 KW)
		e. Jigaon (30 KW)
18. (a) Nearest Railway-head	:	Bhalukpong (100 kms. from Bomdila)

	(b) Nearest Airport	:	Salonibari, Tezpur (160 kms. from Bomdila)
19.	Altitude of Circle & District Headquarters (in metres)	:	a. Bomdila varying from 2430 to 2700 b. Dirang-1407 c. Kalaktang-1113 d. Nafra-1790 e. Thrizino-1224 f. Bhalukpong-213
20.	Important Tourist Spot	:	a. Rupa b. Bomdila c. Dirang d. Sela Pass
21.	Known occurrence of minerals	:	(a) Coal-Near Bhairab Kund and Kameng Bari (b) Copper Ore-near Dirang (c) Dolomite-in Dedza & Rupa area (d) Glass sand-in Rupa area (e) Marble-in Dirang area
22.	Important Forest Species	:	Blue Pine, Chir Pine Sopa, Hollock, Cupressus, Jutali, Hingoli, Amari, Dhuna, Gomari, Bonsum and Walnut
23.	Important Fauna		
	a. Mammalia	:	Leopard, Jungle Cat, Jackal, Leopard Cat,

		Indian Elephant, Barking Bear, Indian Wild Bear, Musk Deer, Monkey, Red Panda.
b. Birds	:	Babblers, Warblers, Chats, Jungle Fowls, Black-Neasted Kaleege, Hornbill, Green and Indian Pigeon.
24. Landuse Pattern	:	Forest, Jhumming, TRC, WRC and Horticulture.
25. Main Agriculture Produces	:	Wheat, Buck Wheat, Barley, Maize, Millet, Rajma, Potato, Soybean.
26. Main Horticulture Produces	:	Apple, Pears, Plum, Orange.
27. Main Livestocks	:	Yak, Sheep, Pig, Pony, Cattle, Mithun and Goat.

Education

As per the census of 1991 the district occupies a significant position taking the total literacy percentage into consideration with a total population of 56,421 (7th in the order of total population of the respective districts.) The district has got 36.48% of literacy, second in the literacy rate, first being the Lohit district having 39.4%. So far as the male and female literacy rate in the state is concerned, West Kameng comes to the third position in both projecting 44.72 percent and 27.06 percent respectively. Moreover, the district's decennial growth rate of population (1981-91) seems to be ideal, i.e. 35.74 slight below the state's growth rate of 35.86.

Table 5.1: Administrative Setup Showing District Sub-Division and Circle in West Kameng District

Name of the District	*Name of the Sub-division*	*Name of Circle*	*Year of Opening*	*Rank of Officer Incharge*
West Kameng	BOMDILA	Bomdila	1953	Deputy Commissioner
		Dirang	1954	Extra Asstt. Commissioner
		Nafra	1954	Circle Officer
	THRIZINO	Thrizino	1953	Sub-Divisional Officer
		Jamiri	1994	Circle Officer
		Bhalukpong	1973	Extra Asstt. Commissioner
	RUPA	Rupa	1990	Sub-Divisional Officer
		Kalaktang	1954	Extra Asstt. Commissioner
		Singchung	1997	Extra Asstt. Commissioner

Source: Deputy Commissioner, Bomdila.

Against the backdrop of such literacy data the district needs special attention in the field of higher education. Though the district has a degree college at its headquarters, Bomdila, covering the students of its catchment areas of three districts, West Kameng, East Kameng and Tawang, it sends a very few students for further higher education, the details will be discussed later in this chapter.

District and Lower Level Organization Setup

'District' being the primary unit of planning and management of education, each of the eleven districts has a setup of educational inspectorate under the charge of a Deputy Director of Public Instruction (re-designed as the Deputy

Table 5.2: Distance of Circle from District Headquarters

District Headquarters	*Circle Headquarters*	*Distance from District HQ (KM)*	*Means of Communication*
BOMDILA	Bomdila	0.0	
	Dirang	42.0	
	Kalaktang	99.0	
	Bhalukpong	100.0	APSTS/
	Nafra	55.0	Private Bus
	Thrizino	127.0	
	Jameri	35.0	
	Singchung	27.0	

Source: Deputy Commissioner/Station Superintendent, APSTS, Bomdila.

Director of School Education—DDSE), as shown in figure 5.1. For his assistance there are field officers like District Adult Education Officers (DAEOs), Assistant District Education Officers (ADEOs), Adult Education Supervisors (AES) and supportive staff and group and staff for the inspection/supervision and effective management of various educational activities. DAEO is mainly responsible for the Adult Education delegated to him by the Government. He draws programme in the district besides looking after the office in the absence of the DDSE. He also exercises financial powers and disburses the salary of staff posted at the district level. ADEOs and Adult Education Supervisors assist the DDSE in inspection/supervision. They are also responsible for various reports and returns in respect of the schools in the block under their charge. Each block in the state has been provided either with an ADEO or an Adult Education Supervisor to look after the educational activities.

The DDSE, being busy in the office dealing with day to day administration mainly with financial and establishment matters, hardly finds time to inspect schools in the district.

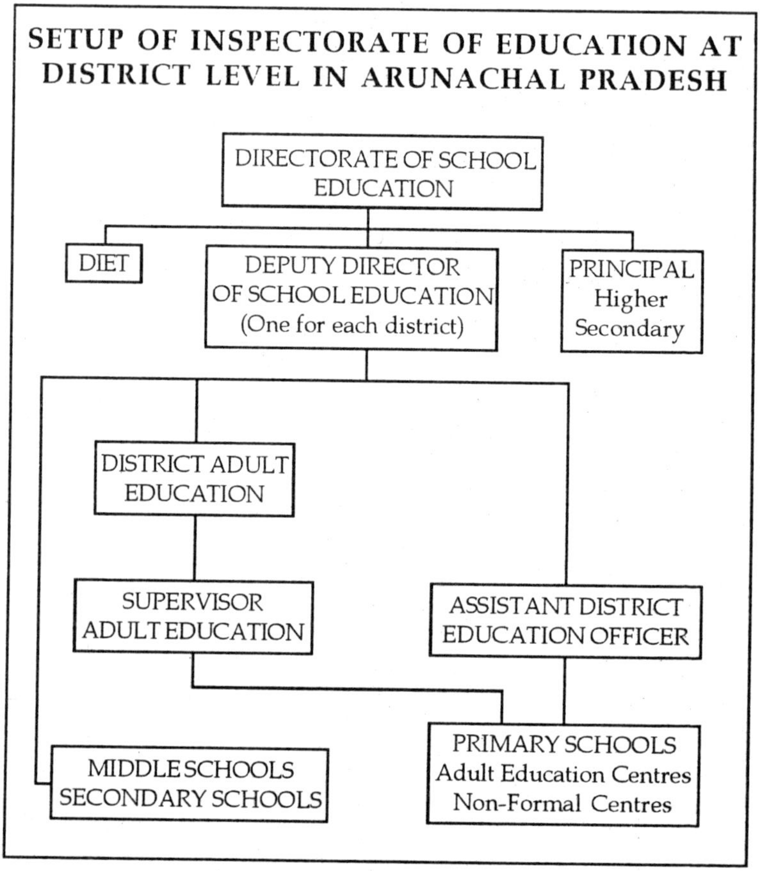

Figure 5.1

The scheme of school complexes has been adopted in the state since 1988-89 and for the effective implementation of the scheme, a district level committee is constituted under the Chairmanship of DC/ADC.

Role of Local Bodies

In Arunachal Pradesh local bodies play a significant role in educational administration in a restricted sense of the term. They have certain powers but do not have any organisational machinery to either scrutinise and execute any educational proposal/program or supervise/inspect educational institutions. However, these bodies do have certain educational responsibilities. For instance, if a school is needed by a particular village or group of village under a Gram Panchayat, the latter keeping in view certain specified conditions, submits a proposal to the Anchal Samity for taking necessary action. The conditions are : (a) The village(s) under the particular Gram Panchayat have to allot sufficient land at a suitable location for the proposed school and also provide playground for children, (b) The villagers have to build the school buildings and hostels, if required, for students and residential quarters for the teaching and not-teaching staff of the proposed school, with locally available materials and also maintain the buildings till the government constructs 'pucca' or 'semi-pucca' buildings; and (c) the villagers have to provide adequate number of children of both the sexes, for utilising the facilities of the school.

Once the school is built and starts functioning, the Gram Panchayat ensures its smooth functioning, maintains strict vigil over it and meets its requirements, as and when demanded by the school. It neither interferes in the running of the school nor inspects it. If the school does not function properly the Gram Panchayat brings the matter to the notice of the concerned Inspector of the School of the Anchal Samity. It may hence be said that other than building schools and ensuring their smooth functioning by keeping a strict vigil from outside, the Gram Panchayats and Anchal Samitis have not other function or duty related to educational administration.

Since education in its broader sense means an all-round development of the individual Anchal Samities may be said to be meeting educational/developmental needs of the villagers because they carry out directly and at times indirectly, certain responsibilities regarding the spread of education and educational management such as:

- Maintaining community radio sets for the benefit of the rural people;
- Establishing and maintaining library, reading rooms, clubs and other places for recreation and games;
- Popularising sports in the villages, organising and celebrating national and other festivals and functions;
- Spreading education through English medium;
- Establishing and maintaining theatres for the promotion of art and culture;
- Propagating ideas like installation of smokeless chullahs, provisions of proper ventilation in houses;
- Organising welfare activities for women, children and literate people as also for upliftment of the backward and underprivileged sections of the society; and
- Organising voluntary labour for community work and upliftment of the villages.

Thus, though the government agencies are actually vested with powers in relation to educational management and development, different tiers of the Panchayat Raj System carry on these functions indirectly with the help and co-operation of the local community, which in different districts and at the grass-root level make provisions for schools and other educational facilities.

It is pertinent here to throw light on the educational infrastructure available with the West Kameng District. Tables dealing with various aspects of the infrastructure in a decade could suffice the objective of the study.

Table 5.4a shows that within a decade (1989-90 to 1998-99) the number of both government and non-government educational institutions has increased substantially according to the rising need of the students, i.e., the number of pre-primary schools has increased from 29 in 1989-90 to 36 in 1998-99, an increase of 21%, the primary school from 79 to

Table 5.3: Yearwise Distribution of Government (Arunachal Pradesh) and Non-Government (Other than Arunachal Government) Educational Institutions in West Kameng (1989-90 to 1998-99)

Sl. No.	Year	No. of Insitutions																		Remarks
		College			Higher Sec. School			Secondary School			Middle School			Primary School			Pre-Primary School			
		G	NT	T	G	NG	T	G	NG	T	G	NG	T	G	NG	T	G	NG	T	
1	2	3	4	5	6	7	8	9	10	11	12	13	14	15	16	17	18	19	20	21
1.	1989-90	1*	–	1	1	1	2	6	–	6	12	1	13	78	1	79	27	2	29	
2.	1990-91	1	–	1	1	1	2	7	1	8	11	1	12	83	4	37	28	1	29	
3.	1991-92	1	–	1	1	1	2	7	1	8	12	1	13	90	4	94	28	2	30	
4.	1992-93	1	–	1	1	1	2	7	1	8	16	1	17	101	4	105	26	2	28	
5.	1993-94	1	–	1	2	1	3	7	1	8	15	1	16	111	4	115	30	2	32	
6.	1994-95	1	–	1	3	1	4	6	1	7	17	1	18	96	4	100	30	2	32	
7.	1995-96	1	–	1	3	1	4	5	1	6	15	1	16	94	4	98	30	2	32	
8.	1996-97	1	–	1	4	1	5	6	1	7	16	1	17	99	8	107	32	2	34	
9.	1997-98	1	–	1	4	1	5	6	1	7	18	3	21	98	8	106	33	2	35	
10.	1998-99	1	–	1	4	1	5	6	1	7	18	3	21	98	8	106	34	2	36	

* Established in March 1988.

G = Government, NG = Non-government, T = Total.

Source: Collected and compiled from District Statistical Handbook of West Kameng, D.S.O., Bomdila.

Table 5.4: Decennial Growth Rate of Institutions

Types of Institutions	*No. in 1989-90*	*No. in 1998-99*	*%age (increase)*
Pre-primary	29	36	21
Primary	79	106	34
Middle	13	21	62
Secondary	06	07	17
Higher Secondary	02	05	150
College	01	01	Nil
Total	**130**	**176**	**35**

Source: Abstract from the Table 5.4.

106, an increase of 34%, in the middle schools from 13 to 21, an increase of 62%, the secondary schools from 06 to 07, an increase of 17%, the higher secondary schools from 02 to 05, an increase of 150%, and the number of college has remained the same because the need to increase the same has not been felt even necessary due to the low students strength and load of the college. The table also reflects that the initiative from the side of the Government as well as from the public has been significant in opening up and upgrading the school since there has been an increase of 35% in the growth of institutions. Mention may be made, the increase of the educational institution by stage in percentage over the decade has been as low as 17% in secondary level and as higher as 150% in higher secondary level. This unusual difference seems to have occurred due to the fact that less number of middle schools have been upgraded to secondary schools against more number of secondary schools upgraded into higher secondary ones during the said decade.

In the Table 5.5 is shown the students' as well as the teachers' strength over the last decade (1989-90 to 1998-99) right from the pre-primary to the college levels. Table 5.5a shows the decennial growth rate of students, teachers and their ratio over the same discussed decade. In the pre-primary level there is a decrease of 39% in the enrolment of

Table 5.5: Yearwise Distribution of Students and Teachers' Strength in both Government (Arunachal Pradesh) and Non-government (Other Than Arunachal Government) Educational Institutions of West Kameng (1989-90 to 1998-99)

Sl. No.	No. of Institutions (Govt. and Non-govt.)																		
	Year	*College*			*Higher Sec. School*			*Secondary School*			*Middle School*			*Primary School*			*Pre-primary School*		
		No. of Students	No. of Teachers	Teacher Student Ratio	No. of Students	No. of Teachers	Teacher Student Ratio	No. of Students	No. of Teachers	Teacher Student Ratio	No. of Students	No. of Teachers	Teacher Student Ratio	No. of Students	No. of Teachers	Teacher Student Ratio	No. of Students	No. of Teachers	Teacher Student Ratio
1	*2*	*3*	*4*	*5*	*6*	*7*	*8*	*9*	*10*	*11*	*12*	*13*	*14*	*15*	*16*	*17*	*18*	*19*	*20*
1.	1989-90	143	4	1:36	1461	65	1:22	1726	87	1:20	1417	80	1:18	3325	154	1:22	1045	36	1:29
2.	1990-91	111	4	1:28	1614	69	1:23	1952	96	1:26	1405	86	1:16	4332	188	1:23	962	30	1:32
3.	1991-92	142	9	1:16	1877	60	1:31	2380	109	1:22	1655	80	1:21	4074	188	1:22	1054	33	1:32
4.	1992-93	126	13	1:10	1836	74	1:25	2527	1114	1:22	2166	115	1:19	4024	183	1:22	1074	34	1:32
5.	1993-94	102	13	1:8	1851	99	1:19	2455	118	1:21	2104	124	1:17	4185	194	1:22	1146	39	1:29
6.	1994-95	109	14	1:8	2418	107	1:23	1854	109	1:17	2283	122	1:19	3954	208	1:19	1216	37	1:33
7.	1995-96*	127	16	1:8	3794**	176	–	–	–	–	1729	96	1:18	3295	187	1:18	–	–	–
8.	1996-97	160	15	1:11	3217	140	1:23	1696	89	1:19	1821	102	1:18	4321	227	1:19	1018	15	1:68
9.	1997-98	135	15	1:9	2295	112	1:20	1586	79	1:20	2444	107	1:23	5261	175	1:30	1232	21	1:59
10.	1998-99	152	15	1:11	2457	112	1:22	1644	79	1:21	2151	96	1:22	2764	165	1:17	638	21	1:30

* Handbook for 1995-96 not published, data collected from the manuscript, D.S.O., Bomdila.

** Both secondary and higher secondary.

Source: Collected and compiled from the *Statistical Handbooks of West Kameng District,* District Statistical Office, Bomdila, Offices of the DDSE and the Principal, Government College, Bomdila.

Table 5.5a: Decennial Growth Rate of Students, Teachers and Their Ratio

Type of Institution	*1989-90*			*1998-99*			*%age change*			*Change ratio of teachers & students over the decade*	
	No. of students	*No. of teachers*	*Teacher pupil ratio*	*No. of students*	*No. of teachers*	*Teacher pupil ratio*	*No. of students*	*No. of teachers*	*Teacher pupil ratio*	*Increase %age*	*Decrease %age*
1	*2*	*3*	*4*	*5*	*6*	*7*	*8*	*9*	*10*	*11*	*12*
Pre-primary	1045	36	1:29	638	21	1:30	(–) 39	(–) 42	(+) 03		27
Primary	3325	154	1:22	2764	165	1:17	(–) 17	(+) 07	(–) 23	51	
Middle	1417	80	1:18	2151	96	1:22	(+) 52	(+) 20	(+) 22	46	
Secondary	1726	87	1:20	1644	79	1:21	(–) 05	(+) 09	(+) 05		10
Higher Secondary	1461	65	1:22	2457	112	1:22	(+) 68	(+) 72	NIL	21	
College	143	04	1:36	162	15	1:11	(+) 13	(+) 275	(–) 69	07	
Total	**9117**	**426**	**1:21**	**9816**	**494**	**1:20**	**(+) 8**	**(+) 16**	**(–) 05**	**10**	

* Ratio of the teachers' and students' strength over the decade is fixed as follows:
For example: For pre-primary level = (No. of students enrolled in the 1998-99) – (No. of students enrolled in 1989-90) ÷ (No. of teachers' strength in 1998-99) – (No. of teachers' strength in 1989-90)

the students, a decrease of 42% in the teaching strength but there is a slightly increase of 3% in the teacher-pupil ratio and a decrease of 27% in the ratio of increase of teaching strength in comparison to the increase students strength. Despite an increase of pre-primary institutions by 21% (Table 5.4a), there has been a decreasing tendency in the enhancement of students and teaching strength. This trend might have been due to the larger enrolment of nursery students in the other type of institutions expecting in the pre-primary ones or due to the parents' disinterest to send their wards to the said institutions. Again the decrease of teachers' strength might have occurred due to their transfer from the pre-primary to primary schools basing on the fact that the teacher-pupil ratio has almost remained equal with a little variation of 3%. Almost same kind of trend has been reflected in the secondary level. But a very significant line of increase in all areas is clearly visible in the middle school, higher secondary and college levels. There have been the spectacular growth ratios of 51% and 46% respectively in the primary and middle school levels of the increase of teachers' strength in comparison to the increase of students' strength. Moreover, one uncommon figure of +27.5% is seen on the increase of teachers strength in the college in the 1998-99 against the same in 1989-90 is due to the fact that in 1989-90 there were only six subjects taught in the college without Honours. Later next year, Honours Course was introduced in three subjects, hence demand for the strength of the teachers increase substantially. Even for other pass subjects more teachers were also appointed.

The figures of teacher-pupil ratios at different stages of school education in the district and above all the average teacher-pupil ratio over the decade (1:20) seem to imply that since the ratio is quite low compared to the national figure (1:30), the quality of education imparted should be high. With this kind of teachers towards the students and moreover, remedial teaching for weak students too becomes a feasible possibility in this context.

Table 5.6: Existing Building Position, Deployment List and Enrolment as in July'98 of the Types of Institutions of the Different Circles

Sl. No.	*Name of the College/School*	*Existing Building/No. of Pucca/Lt. ILC/HT/SPT/OBT*				*Deployment List*				*Enrolment*	*Remarks*
		No. of Rooms	*No. of Boys*	*Hostels Girls*	*Teacher's Quarters*	*No. of Teachers*	*Designation*	*Qualification*	*T/UT*	*Total Boys/Girls*	
1	2	3	4	5	6	7	8	9	10	11	12
A.	**Bomdila**										
1.	Govt. College Bomdila*	17 Pucca-4 SPT-13	01 (SPT) 22 seats	–	Type V-I III-5, I-10 Bachelor Barrack-7 Nos (7-pucca) (17-SPT)	16	Principal-1 Senior Lect.-5 Lecturer-10	MA-5 MA M.Phil-4 MA PhD-2 MA M.Phil, PhD NET-2	–	162 $\frac{124}{38}$	* At present the college runs in a temporary building. It is expected, it may develop a permanent campus of its own in near future.
2.	Govt. Higher Sec. School, Bomdila	30 (SPT) Auditor-ium 26 Sc. Lab.	6 blocks 26 rooms	1 block 9 rooms	Type V-3 Nos IV-2 Nos III-7 Nos, 11-7 I-2	27	Principal-1 V.P.-1, ST-11 JT-13, ATA-01	–	22-T 5-UT		
3.	Govt. M.E. School, Kakaling	MIBT Blds 10 Rooms OBT-01 Room	–	–	Type II-4 B/Brk-1 (2 Units)	12	JT-5 ATA-7	M.Sc-1 B.Com-1 BA-5 XI-4, X-1	ALL UT		

4.	Govt. Pry. School (GPS) Bomdila	12 (SPT)	–	–	Type-II 1 No.	16	JT-4 ATA-11 ATB-01	MA-1 BA-3 XI-11 UMT-01	ALL UT	$272\frac{139}{133}$	
5.	Govt. Pry. School, New Bomdila	02 (Pucca)	–	–	Type-I (OBT) 1 No.	05	AT(SG)-01 ATA-03 ATB-01	XII-2 X-2 UMT-1	ALL UT	$59\frac{27}{22}$	
6.	G.P.S. Bank Colony, Bomdila	07 (OBT)	–	–	Type-III 1 No.	09	AT(SG)-1 JT-1 ATA-6 ATB-1	B.Sc-1 BA-2 XII-2 X-2	ALL UT	$181\frac{95}{86}$	
7.	G.M.S. Upper Gompa, Bomdila	07 (SPT)	–	–	Type-I, 1 No. (OBT)	05	JT-2 ATA-3	M.Sc, B.Ed-1 MA-1, BA-1 XII-2	T-1 UT-4	61 only boys	School building produced by the Buddhist Cultural Society, Bomdila.
8.	G.P.S., Wango	04 (SPT)	–	–	Type-II, 1 No. (SPT) Type-I, 1 No. (OBT)	01	AT(SG)	–	UT	$71\frac{43}{31}$	
9.	G.P.S., Sera Village	03 (Pucca)	–	–	Type-I, 1 No. (OBT)	04	JT-1 ATA-2 AT(SG)-1	MA, B.Ed-1 XII-2 X-1	T-1 UT-3	$45\frac{20}{25}$	

B. Bhalukpong Circle										
1. Govt. Sec. School, Bhalukpong	6-Pucca 5-SPT 4-OBT	4 Rooms OBT	4 Rooms Pucca	SPT-II-5 Pucca-II-2 Pucca-I-6	14	HM-1, JT-6 ATA-6 PTI-1	BA, B.Ed-1 BA-9, B.Sc-2 XII-2	T-1 UT-13	$416\frac{232}{184}$	
2. G.P.S., Lower Bhalukpong	2-SPT 4-OBT	–	–	OBT-II-2	06	JT-3 ATA-3	BA, B.Ed-1 BA, BT-1 BA-3, XII-1	T-2 UT-4	$157\frac{89}{68}$	
3. G.P.S., Tippi	2-SPT 1-HT, 4-OBT	–	–	OBT-II-2	03	JT-1 ATA-2	BA-1 X-2	UT	$91\frac{51}{42}$	
4. G.P.S., Kamengbari	4-OBT	–	–	OBT-II-1 OBT-I-1	02	ATA-2	B.Sc, X	UT	$63\frac{32}{31}$	
5. G.P.S., Doimora	6-SPT	–	–	OBT-II-6	02	JT, ATB	BA, UMT	UT	$35\frac{19}{16}$	
C. Dirang Circle										
1. Govt. Higher Sec. School, Dirang	19-SPT Audi-torium Sc. Lab.	2-7 blocks	1-3 blocks	Type-III-4 Type-II-11	27	P-1, VP-1 ST-6 JT-10 AT-5 PTI-1	M.Sc, B.Ed-2 MA, B.Ed-11 MA-1, M.Sc-1 B.Sc, B.Ed-3 BA-5, XII-4	T-16 UT-11	$598\frac{327}{271}$	SPT-I to IV under construc-tion.
2. Govt. Sec. School, Namshu	12-SPT 5-MIBT	1-SPT	2-OBT	Type-II-2 Type-I-2	10	HM-1 JT-7 ATA-1 PTI-1	MA, BT-1 MA-1, MA B.Ed-1 M.Sc, Lt-1, XII-1 BA-2, BA B.Ed-2	T-4 UT-6		
3. G.M.S., Man-dalaphudung	6-HT	1-HT	Type-II-2 (Deplorable)	05	JT-1 ATA-4	B.Com, BA B.Sc, XII, X	UT			

4.	G.M.S., Nyukmadung	4-HT 2-OBT	1-HT	1-OBT	SPT-II-2 HT-II-2, OBT-I-1	04	JT-3 ATA-1	B.Sc-2, BA-1	UT		
5.	G.M.S., Dirang Village	4-SPT 5-HT	1-SPT 3 Rooms	–	SPT-II-4 OBT-I-1	07	JT-5 ATA-2	MA, B.Ed, M.Sc, BA, B.Sc, XII	T-1 UT-6		SPT-II-2 under construction.
6.	G.M.S., Sangti	8-SPT 1-OBT	1-OBT	1-OBT	SPT-II-3 OBT-I-3 B/Barrack-2	07	JT-2 ATA-2 ATB-2 ATC-1	MA, BA, BA B.Ed, B.Sc, XII,	T-1 UT-6		SPT boys hostel for 20 boarders under construction.
7.	G.M.S., Salari	6-SPT 1-OBT	1-OBT	–	OBT-II-6	06	JT (SG)-1 JT-4, ATA-1	MA, M.Sc, BA B.Ed, BA BT, X	T-2 UT-4		
8.	G.M.S., Thembang	3-ILC 2-OBT	–	–	OBT-II-2 OBT-I-1	03	JT-3	MA, M.Sc, BA	UT		ILC-5 rooms under construction.
9.	G.P.S., Senge	3-SPT	–	–	HT-II-2	02	JT-1, AT-1	BA, XII	UT	75, 45/30	
10.	G.P.S., Manpe	2-LT	–	–	OBT-I-1	01	Run by community worker		UT	13,9/4	
11.	G.P.S., Dundri	2-SPT	–	–	OBT-I-1	01	ATA	XII	UT	12,6/6	
12.	G.P.S., Melongkong	2-LT 2-OBT	–	–	SPT-II-2	02	JT, ATA	BA, XII	UT	49,24/25	
13.	G.P.S., Ramacamp	3-SPT	–	–	–	03	JT, ATA ATB	BA, XII, UMT	UT	50, 25/25	
14.	G.P.S. Chug.	6-MIBT	–	–	OBT-1	02	JT, ATA	M.Sc, XII	UT	38, 19/19	

15.	G.P.S., Lish	6-SPT	–	–	MIBT-I-2	02	JT, ATA	B.Sc, B.Ed, XII	T-1, UT-1	41,36-5
16.	G.P.S., Lism Gompache	3-LT	–	–	OBT-1	02	ATA-2	XII, X	UT	32, 23/9
17.	G.P.S., Lubrang	3-SPT	–	–	–	01	ATA	BA	UT	17, 12/5
18.	G.P.S. Jyotinagar	2-OBT	–	–	–	02	ATA-2	XII-2	UT	31, 20/22
19.	G.P.S., Yewang	4-SPT	–	–	SPT-I-2, OBT-I-2	06	JT-3, ATA-3	BA-3, XII-3	UT	127, 60/67
20.	G.P.S.,	2-OBT	–	–	OBT-I-2 B/Brk-2	01	ATA	XII	UT	25, 17/8
21.	G.P.S., Namthung	2-LT	–	–	OBT-I-2 B/Brk-2	02	ATA-2	BA, XII	UT	35, 11/24
22.	G.P.S., Khalibok	2-LT	–	–	–	01	ATA	MA, B.Ed	T	17, 13/4
23.	G.P.S., Khasso	2-OBT	–	–	–	01	ATA	BA	UT	20, 10/10
24.	G.P.S., Bishumphudung	3-OBT 2-LT	–	–	OBT-I-1	01	ATB	XII	UT	29, 12/17
25.	G.P.S., Sagar	2-OBT 2-LT	–	–	OBT-I-1	02	ATA	XII-1	UT	11, 7/4
26.	G.P.S., Varshipam	3-ILC	–	–	OBT-I-1	01	ATA	XII	UT	22, 3/19

27.	G.P.S., Munna Camp	2-LT 3-Pucca	–	–	–	02	ATA	XII-2	UT	38, 17/21
28.	G.P.S., Cherrong	2-SPT	–	–	OBT-I-2	01	ATA	XII	UT	20, 11/9
29.	G.P.S., Chander	3-ILC	–	–	OBT-I-2	01	ATA	XII	UT	15, 7/8
30.	G.P.S., Lagam	3-SPT	–	–	OBT-I-1	01	ATB	UMT	UT	4, 4/0
31.	G.P.S., Semnak	2-LT	–	–	–	01	ATA	XII	UT	10, 3/7
32.	G.P.S., Pangma	2-LT	–	–	OBT-I-1	01	ATA	BA	UT	16, 5/11
33.	G.P.S., Gongthung	3-ILC	–	–	–	01	ATA	BA	UT	4, 1/3
34.	G.P.S., Darbu	1-LT	–	–	OBT-I-1	02	ATA	BA, XII	UT	11, 6/5
35.	G.P.S., Rahung	6-SPT	–	–	SPT-II-2	02	JT, ATA	BA	UT	26, 17/9
36.	G.P.S., Rahung Powerhouse	3-OBT	–	–	–	01	ATA	XII	UT	18, 10/8
37.	G.P.S., Warjong	2-LT	–	–	SPT-II-1	02	JT-2	BA	UT	16, 11/5
38.	G.P.S., Khellong Bamrok	2-LT	–	–	OBT-I-2	02	ATA-2	X	UT	26, 12/14

D. Jamiri Circle									
1. Govt. Middle School, Buragaon	6-MIBT	5-MIBT	–	MIBT-II-6	03	ATA	MA, XII, X	UT	
2. G.P.S., Circle HQ, Jamiri	2-SPT	–	–	OBT-I-1	02	ATB-2	X	UT	54, 27/27
3. G.P.S., Jamiri Village	4-SPT	–	–	SPT-1 OBT-II-1	02	ATA-2	XII	UT	
4. G.P.S., I.V. School New Kaspi	2-SPT 1-OBT	1-OBT	–	OBT-II-1 Type-I-1	03	JT-2 ATA-1	B.Sc B.Ed, MA B.Ed, XII	T-2 UT-1	72, 40/32
5. G.P.S., Dahung	2-OBT	–	–	–	01	ATB	X	UT	28, 14/14
6. G.P.S., Namfri	2-SPT	–	–	OBT-I-1	01	ATA	X	UT	14, 5/9
7. G.P.S., Tenga Valley	7-SPT	–	–	OBT-II-2	04	JT, ATA-2 ATC-1	BA-2, XII, UMT	UT	115, 66/49
8. G.P.S., Ramalingam	2-SPT	–	–	OBT-II-1	02	JT, ATB	BA, UMT	UT	40, 16/24
E. Kalaktang Circle									
1. Govt. Hr. Sec. School, Kalaktang	21-SPT	4-SPT Blocks	2-SPT Blocks	SPT-II-9 SPT-I-5	30	–	–	T-16 UT-14	–
2. Govt. Sec. School, Shergaon	13-SPT 2-OBT	–	SPT-1	SPT-II-4 OBT-I-2 B/Brk-4	14	HM-1, JT-6 ATA-4, ATB-2 ATA-1	MA, B.Ed-3 M.Sc-2, BA-3 XII-3, UMT-3	T-2 UT-12	416, 232/184

3.	G.M.S., Boha	5-SPT	–	–	B/Brk-4	05	JT-3, ATA-2	M.Sc-1, BA-2 B.Com-1, XII-1	UT	
4.	G.M.S.,	7-SPT	–	–	SPT-II-2	05	JT-3, ATA-2	MA B.Ed, MA,XII,BA-2	T-1 UT-4	
5.	G.M.S., Morsing	7-SPT	–	–	SPT-II-2	05	JT-3, ATA-2	B.Com, BA XII-2,B.ScB.Ed	T-1 UT-4	
6.	G.M.S., Balemu	3-SPT	–	–	B/Brk-5	05	JT-3, ATA-2	MA, BABT,X B.ScB.Ed, BA	T-1 UT-4	
7.	G.M.S., Jigaon	5-SPT	–	–	SPT-II-2	07	JT-3, ATA-3 ATB-1	MA,B.Sc,BA, X,BABT,XII-2	T-1 UT-6	
8.	G.P.S., Angkaling	3-SPT	–	–	SPT-II-2	02	JT, ATA	BA, XII	UT	25, 14/11
9.	G.P.S., Betchelling	3-SPT	–	–	SPT-I-2	01	ATA	XII	UT	14, 8/6
10.	G.P.S., Lungdur	3-SPT	–	–	SPT-I-2	02	JT, ATA	MA, XII	UT	32, 19/13
11.	G.P.S., Lephakpu	3-SPT	–	–	SPT-I-2	02	ATB, ATC	UMT	UT	6, 3/3
12.	G.P.S., Brok-palengchen	3-SPT	–	–	SPT-II-1	01	ATA	BA	UT	12, 7/5
13.	G.P.S., Kamalangchen	3-SPT	–	–	SPT-II-1	02	JT	MA B.Ed	T	42, 19/23
14.	G.P.S., Samphung	3-SPT	–	–	SPT-I-2	02	JT, ATA	MA B.Ed, MA	T-1 UT-1	32, 12/20

15. G.P.S., KTG Village	3-SPT	–	–	SPT-I-2	03	JT-2, ATA	B.Sc B.Ed, B.Sc, X	T-1 UT-2	36, 10/26
16. G.P.S., Chengi	3-SPT	–	–	SPT-II-1	02	JT, ATA	BA, XII	UT	13, 3/10
17. G.P.S., Samdung	3-SPT	–	–	SPT-II-1	01	JT	BA	UT	12, 3/9
18. G.P.S., Warrangpam	2-SPT	–	–	SPT-II-1	01	ATA	BA	UT	6, 0/6
19. G.P.S., Painaktang	3-SPT	–	–	SPT-II-2	02	JT, ATA	BA, X	UT	34, 8/26
20. G.P.S., Domkho	2-SPT	–	–	SPT-I-1	01	ATA	XII	UT	12, 8/4
21. G.P.S., Rong-thorjarpam	2-SPT	–	–	SPT-I-1	01	ATA	M.Sc	UT	13, 10/3
22. G.P.S., Sangeim	2-SPT	–	–	SPT-I-1	01	ATA	XII	UT	26, 14/12
23. G.P.S., Waizer	2-SPT	–	–	SPT-I-1	01	ATB	UMT	UT	13, 6/7
24. G.P.S., Yelongripam	2-SPT	–	–	SPT-I-1	01	ATA	XII	UT	15, 11/4
F. Nafra Circle									
1. Govt. Sec. School Nafra	10-SPT & HT	SPT-4 Blocks	SPT-4 Blocks	Type-III-2 Type-II-6	13	HM-1, JT-8 ATA-2 PTI, ATB	MA BT, MA B.Sc, XII, X, BA-5, B.ScB.Ed-2	T-4 UT-9	219, 119/100

2.	G.M.S., Dibbin	4-HT	2-OBT	2-OBT	SPT-II-2	03	JT-2, ATA	B.ScB.Ed, BA-2	T-1 UT-2	
3.	G.M.S., Jerigaon	10-SPT	–	–	SPT-II-3	04	JT, ATA-2, ATB	BA, MA-2 UMT	UT	
4.	G.P.S., L/Dzong	3-HT	–	–	SPT-I-1	01	JT	BA	UT	18, 8/10
5.	G.P.S., U/Dzong	3-SPT	–	–	–	01	JT	BA	UT	16, 8/8
6.	G.P.S., Khellong	2-SPT	–	–	SPT-I-1	01	ATA	BA	UT	13, 8/5
7.	G.P.S., Nizung	2-OBT	–	–	SPT-I-1	01	JT	M.Sc	UT	12, 5/7
8.	G.P.S., Khazalong	2-HT	2-OBT	2-OBT	SPT-I-2	03	ATA-2, ATB	BA, XII, UMT	UT	14, 8/6
9.	G.P.S., Khellong Medical Colony	2-OBT	–	–	SPT-I-2	02	JT	BA	UT	38, 19/19
10.	G.P.S., Saidle	2-HT	–	–	OBT-I-1	02	JT	BA	UT	22, 13/9
11.	G.P.S., Khoina	2-LT	–	–	OBT-I-1	01	ATA	XII	UT	29, 12/17
12.	G.P.S., Bichhom IV	2-SPT	2-OBT	2-OBT	OBT-I-1	02	ATA	BA, XII	UT	38, 20/18
13.	G.P.S., Rurang	2-OBT	–	–	OBT-I-1	01	ATA	X	UT	22, 14/8
14.	G.P.S., Mathow	2-OBT	–	–	HT-II-2	01	ATA	XII	UT	16, 10/6

15. G.P.S., Dibrik	2-HT	–	–	HT-2	01	ATA	BA	UT	23, 11/12
16. G.P.S., Nakhu	3-HT	–	–	HT-2	02	ATA	XII, X	UT	22, 14/8
17. G.P.S., Nachibon	3-HT	–	–	HT-2	02	ATA	XII	UT	19, 11/8
18. G.P.S., Ditchik	3-HT	–	–	HT-2	01	ATA	BA	UT	16, 10/6
19. G.P.S., Janaching	2-OBT	–	–	Type-I-1	01	ATA	M.Sc	UT	30, 17/13
G. Rupa Circle									
1. Govt. Hr. Sec. School Rupa	22-SPT	1-Block	–	SPT-III-7 SPT-II-6 B/Brk-4 OBT-I-2	28	Prl., VP, ST-10 JT-14 ATA-2	MA B.Ed-5, B.Sc.-1, M.Sc B.Ed-5, BA B.Ed-3, MABT-1 BA-6, B.Com BT-1	T-16 UT-12	
2. G.P.S., Birpur	3-SPT	–	–	SPT/Brk-2	03	JT, ATA-2	B.Sc, XII-2	UT	34, 18/16
3. G.P.S., Thungree	6-SPT	–	–	SPT-II-2	03	JT, ATA-2	MA B.Ed, XII-2	T-1 UT-2	46, 21/35
4. G.P.S., Dikshi	2-SPT	–	–	SPT-II-1 OBT-II-2	02	ATA	BA B.Ed, BA	T-1 UT-1	16, 9/7
5. G.P.S., Gorba	2-OBT	–	–	OBT-I-2	01	JT	B.Sc, B.Ed,	T	19, 8/11
6. G.P.S., Mukuthing	2-SPT	–	–	OBT-II-2	02	JT, ATA	BA, B.Ed., BA	T-1 UT-1	23, 9/14

7. G.P.S., Membachur	2-SPT	–	–	OBT-II-2	02	ATA, ATB	XII, UMT	UT	22,10/12
8. G.P.S., Mushaksing	2-SPT	–	–	OBT-II-1	01	ATB	UMT	UT	18,11/7
9. G.P.S., Chillipam	3-SPT	–	–	SPT-1-1 OBT-I-2	03	ATA	XII-2, X-1	UT	59,38/21
10. G.P.S., Lumbaktang IV	3-SPT	OBT-1	–	SPT-II-2 OBT-II-1	02	JT, JTA	BA, B.Ed, XII	T-1 UT-1	27, 9/18
H. Singchung Circle									
1. Govt. Sec. School Singchung	12-SPT	OBT-1	OBT-1	SPT-II-2 B/Brk-4 OBT-Brk-4	16	HM-1, JT-11 ATA-3, PTI-1	MA B.Ed, M.Sc B.Ed, B.Sc B.Ed, MA-3, BA-4, B.Sc-4, XII	T-4 UT-12	452, 277/175
I. Thrizino Circle									
1. Govt. Sec. School	10-SPT	SPT-1 Hall	–	SPT-II-4 OBT-II-3	11	HM, JT-6 ATA-4	MA B.Ed, M.Sc B.Ed, B.Sc B.Ed, BABT, MA, BA-5, XII	T-4 UT-7	171, 104/67
2. Govt. Middle School, Palizi	5-SPT	OBT-1	OBT-1	SPT-I-1 MIBT-II-2 OBT-II-3	05	JT-1 ATA-2 ATB-1	BA, XII,	UT	
3. G.P.S., Yayung	2-SPT	–	–	OBT-I-1	01	ATA	XII	UT	10, 5/5
4. G.P.S., Sakrin	2-SPT	–	–	OBT-I-2	02	JA, ATA	BA, XII	UT	27, 16/11

5.	G.P.S., Kararamu	2-SPT	–	–	OBT-I-1	01	ATA	XII	UT	12, 6/6
6.	G.P.S., Palatary	2-SPT	–	–	OBT-I-2	01	ATA	XII	UT	6, 4/2
7.	G.P.S., Karangania	2-SPT	–	–	OBT-I-1	01	ATA	BA	UT	19, 7/12
8.	G.P.S., Thessa	2-SPT	–	–	OBT-I-1	01	ATA	XII	UT	15, 9/6
9.	G.P.S., Challan	4-SPT	–	–	OBT-I-2	01	JT	BA	UT	12, 9/3
10.	G.P.S., Dizangonia	2-SPT	–	–	OBT-I-1	01	JT	BA	UT	20, 11/9
11.	G.P.S., Subbu	2-SPT	–	–	OBT-II-1	01	ATA	B.Com	UT	29, 20/9

Source: Office of the Deputy Director of School Education (DDSE), Bomdila.
HT-Hill Type, ILC-Improved Log Cabin, LT-Local Type, MIBT-Maintained Improved Base Type, OBT-Ordinary Base Type, SPT-Semi Permanent Type.
Untrained-357-75.64%, Trained-115-24.36%, Total-472.

Table 5.6a: Infrastructural Strength of the Different Categories of Schools in the District in 1998

Sl. No.	*Item*		*Specified Strength*	*Strength Total*	*In %age*
1.	**Trained Teacher**		**115**	**472**	**24.36**
	a. Primary		16	189	08.46
	b. Middle		10	93	10.75
	c. Secondary		19	78	24.36
	d. Hr. Secondary		70	112	62.50
2.	**Untrained Teachers**		**357**	**472**	**75.64**
	a. Primary		173	189	91.54
	b. Middle		83	93	89.25
	c. Secondary		59	78	75.65
	d. Hr. Secondary		42	112	37.5
3.	**Hostels**		**30**	**176**	**17.04**
	a. Primary	I. Boys & Girls	Nil	Nil	Nil
	b. Middle	I. Boys	8	18	44.44
		II. Girls	5	18	27.77
	c. Secondary	I. Boys	5	6	83.33
		II. Girls	5	6	83.33
	d. Hr. Secondary	I. Boys	4	4	100.00
		II. Girls	3	4	75.00
4.	**Single Teacher Schools (Primary Only)**		**47**	**98**	**48.00**
5.	**More Rooms and Less Teachers**		**86**	**131**	**66.15**
6.	**Less Rooms and More Teachers**		**17**	**131**	**12.97**
7.	**Category of School Rooms**				
	a. Pucca & SPT		472	592	70.94
	b. HT, ILC, LT, MIBT & OBT		120	592	29.06
8.	**Teachers' Quarters**		**370**	**472**	**78.38**

Source: Abstract from the Table 5.6.

Table 5.6 gives an account of the infrastructural strength of the different categories of schools of the district in July 1998. The figure of total trained teachers (24.36%0 seems to be very discouraging compared to the figure to the untrained teachers (75.64%). More alarming are the figure of trained teachers in both primary and middle school level which are much less than the total percentage of trained teachers. With this much high percentage of untrained teachers the district is bound to be affected by low quality of school education. Only about one fourth of trained teachers with the percentage of trained teachers being only 8.46 at primary, 10.785 at middle, 24.35 at secondary and 62.5 at higher secondary stage implies a huge stock of untrained teachers which should be a matter of serious concern. Steps may have to be immediately taken for providing training to inservice and untrained teachers and also to meet the needs of future recruitment of the teachers. Moreover, with 21.62% teachers remaining out the government quarters, it is likely to adversely go against the system.

Healthy and sound school environment is a must to help generate in students a perfect academic pursuit and lenience. Class-room aesthetic surroundings, its elegance, various teachers' teaching at regular intervals, their sincerity and dedication, good hosteling and above all, good friendship are the necessary pre-requisite to develop a quality education. But the district with a 17.04% hostels (Table 5.6a) out of the total school strength, 48% primary schools having one teacher only 29.06% HT, ILC, LT, MIBT and OBT schoolrooms fails to project a soothing schooling atmosphere which ultimately may lead to low quality education. The problem of having single teacher in most of the primary schools is innumerable, the details discussed in the next chapter. Hence, the strength of school rooms compared to the teachers strength seems to be inadequate. About 66% (86 out of 131) of schools do have more rooms and less teachers tracing out the fact that sectionwise more and more classes could be adjusted simultaneously for the better learning of the students as well as for the individualised teaching approach; and about 13% (17 out of 131) of schools do have less rooms and more teachers highlighting the fact that at one time different classes could not be engaged even if they had additional teachers. This is but an irreparable loss to the students as well as teachers' potentiality.

Table 5.8 reflects a dismal scenario of the drop-out rates of the students in the district at different stages, right from primary to the under-graduation in the last 5 years, i.e., 1994-95 to 1998-99. At primary level, the total dropout rate fluctuates within 50.95% to 60.69% compared to the dropout rate of total tribal students fluctuating within 58.61% to 64.45%. But one thing clear from the data is that the drop out rate of the tribal students in each year of the study period is more than the total rate, be it the case of the tribal boys or girls. In some years tribal boys and girls are seen dropping out to the percentage of 66.66 and 70.03 respectively. This is but an alarming figure at the primary level. Over the years while the total dropout rate has decreased by 16% from 1994-95 to 1998-99, the rate of the tribal students has decreased only by 6%.

At the middle school level, dropout rates increase more compared to the ratio at the primary. The total dropout rates vary over the said period in between 70.39% to 83.03% and that of the tribal students in between 75.39% to 84.64%. Moreover, the same trend of more dropout rates of tribal boys and girls gets repeated compared to the total figure of boys and girls. Here also, the highest percentage of tribal girls dropped out (85.88) is more than the boys (83.66). But this rate of the tribal students has decreased over the period in comparison to the primary stage. The number of tribal students going for secondary education over the said period is as high as 25 and as low as 15 out of every 100 and that of boys, is 27 and 16, and that of girls is 22 and 14 respectively.

Table 5.7: Enrolment of Students/Arunachalee in the District by Stages from Primary to Undergraduation

	Year	Class-I			Year	Class-V		
		Boys	Girls	Total		Boys	Girls	Total
Primary	1990-91	992/703	845/614	1847/1317	1994-95	438/271	288/184	726/455
	1991-92	1070/711	918/676	2008/1387	1995-96	516/311	381/263	897/574
	1992-93	1179/795	1003/696	2182/1491	1996-97	462/286	403/263	865/549
	1993-94	1128/719	964/665	2092/1384	1997-98	549/243	389/247	938/490
	1994-95	1009/636	816/835	1825/1173	1998-99	452/212	443/242	895/454
			Class-I				Class-VIII	
Middle	1987-88	972-704	891-683	1863/1387	1994-95	176/115	140/98	316/213
	1988-89	1102/798	816/652	1918/1450	1995-96	279/174	157/92	436/266
	1989-90	1076/771	868/636	1944/1397	1996-97	263/156	211/123	474/279
	1990-91	992/703	845/614	1847/1317	1997-98	318/198	220/135	538/324
	1991-92	1090/11	918/676	2008/1387	1998-99	316/164	231/142	547/306
			Class-I				Class-X	
Secondary	1985-86	976-772	811/619	1786/1341	1994-95	56/37	41/25	97/62
	1986-87	994/732	818/558	1812/1290	1995-96	192/125	114/71	306/196
	1987-88	972/704	891/683	1863/1387	1996-97	217/118	157/92	374/210
	1988-89	1102/798	816/652	1918/1450	1997-98	160-86	120/65	280/151
	1989-90	1076/771	868/626	1944/1397	1998-99	199-109	162-85	361-194

			Class-I				Class-XII	
Higher Secondary	1983-84	908/724	782/591	1690/1315	1994-95	89/52	37/27	126/79
	1984-85	861/692	734/569	1595/1261	1995-96	106/51	42/25	148/76
	1985-86	976/722	811/619	1787/1341	1996-97	52/33	28/10	80/43
	1986-87	994/732	818/558	1812/1290	1997-98	56/22	32/12	88/34
	1987-88	972/704	891/638	1863/1387	1998-99	98/50	42/20	140/70
			Class-I				+3 IIIrd Year	
Under-Graduation	1980-81	889/653	776/578	1665/1231	1994-95	8/7	3/2	11/19
	1981-82	916/732	756/545	1672/1277	1995-96	13/9	8/6	21/15
	1982-83	979/791	744/603	1723/1394	1996-97	18/11	13/11	31/22
	1983-84	908/724	782/591	1690/1315	1997-98	14/8	5/4	19/12
	1984-85	816/692	734/569	1595/1261	1998-99	30/24	14/10	44/34

Source: File Records, Establishment Section, Office of the DDSE West Kameng, Bomdila, *District Statistical Handbook (1980-99)*, District Statistical Office, Bomdila and Office of the Principal, Government College, Bomdila.

Table 5.8:* Drop-out Rates of the Students/Arunachalee in the District by Stages for Five Years, w.e.f. 1994-95 to 1998-99

Stages	Year														
	1994-95			1995-96			1996-97			1997-98			1998-99		
	Boys	Girls	Total	Boys	Girls	Total	Boys	Girls	Total	Boys	Girls	Total	Boys	Girls	Total
Primary	55.84t	65.91	60.69	52.66	58.49	55.32	60.81	59.82	60.35	51.32	59.64	55.16	55.20	45.71	50.95
I-V	61.45	70.03	65.45	56.25	61.09	58.61	64.84	62.21	63.17	66.20	62.85	64.59	66.66	54.93	61.29
Middle	81.89	84.28	83.03	74.68	80.75	77.26	75.55	75.69	75.61	67.94	73.96	60.87	71.00	74.83	72.75
I-VIII	83.66	85.65	84.64	78.19	85.88	81.65	79.76	80.35	80.02	73.11	78.01	75.39	76.93	78.99	77.93
Secondary	94.26	94.94	94.57	80.68	86.06	83.11	77.67	82.37	79.92	85.48	85.29	85.40	81.50	81.33	81.43
I-X	94.87	95.96	95.37	82.92	87.27	84.80	83.32	86.53	84.85	89.22	90.03	89.58	85.86	86.42	86.11
Higher**	90.19	95.26	92.54	87.68	94.27	90.72	94.67	96.54	95.52	94.36	96.08	95.14	89.91	95.28	92.48
Secondary I-XII	92.81	95.43	93.99	92.63	95.75	93.97	95.42	98.38	96.79	96.99	97.84	97.36	92.89	97.07	94.05
Under***	99.10	99.61	99.33	98.58	98.94	98.74	98.16	98.25	98.20	98.45	99.36	98.87	96.51	98.09	97.24
Graduation 1-+3 IIIyr	98.92	99.65	99.26	98.77	98.89	98.82	98.60	98.17	98.42	98.89	99.32	99.08	96.53	98.24	98.30

Source: * This table is drawn and computed on the basis of the data given in Table 5.7.

** Higher Secondary in Class Arts, Commerce and Science Streams.

*** Undergraduation includes only Arts Stream, but covering the student from three districts.

t – In the quotient 55.84/61.45, the numerator 55.84 shows the drop-out rate in Boys in total and the denominator shows the drop-out percentage of Arunachalee Boys similar readings may be made for Girls and Total.

Drop-out rate is calculated as follows:

(i) Drop out rate in Primary (from class I to V) for the year 1994-95 is

$$= \frac{(\text{No. of students enrolled in class I in 1990-91}) - (\text{No. of students enrolled in class V in 1994-95})}{\text{No. of students enrolled in class I in 1990-91}} \times 100$$

(ii) Drop out rate in Middle (from class I to VIII) for the year 1994-95 is

$$= \frac{(\text{No. of students enrolled in class I in 1987-88}) - (\text{No. of students enrolled in class VIII in 1994-95})}{\text{No. of students enrolled in class I in 1987-88}} \times 100$$

(iii) Drop out rate in Secondary (from class I to X) for the 1994-95 is

$$= \frac{(\text{No. of students enrolled in class I in 1985-86}) - (\text{No. of students enrolled in class X in 1994-95})}{\text{No. of students enrolled in class I in 1985-86}} \times 100$$

(iv) Drop out rate in Higher Secondary (from class I to XII) for the 1994-95 is

$$= \frac{(\text{No. of students enrolled in class I in 1983-84}) - (\text{No. of students enrolled in class XII in 1994-95})}{\text{No. of students enrolled in class I in 1983-84}} \times 100$$

(v) Drop out rate in Undergraduation (from class I to +3 III year) for the 1994 is

$$= \frac{(\text{No. of students enrolled in class I in 1980-81}) - (\text{No. of students enrolled in class +3 III year in 1994-95})}{\text{No. of students enrolled in class I in 1980-81}} \times 100$$

This ratio does not take into account: (i) Repeaters and (ii) Children who enter the System after Class I.

At the secondary stage, the similar trend is also reflected. The overall dropout rate from 1994-95 to 1998-99 has decreased by 14% which is little higher than the previous stage. Here the tribal students are seen dropping out to a maximum figure of 95.37% in 1994-95 and a minimum of 84.80% the next year and finally reaching at 86.11% in 1998-99. But over the last five years the overall drop-out rate of the tribal students has decreased by 9% compared to its figure at the middle school level. The tribal girls seem to have dropped more than the tribal boys.

The figure shown at the higher secondary stage are quite alarming and seem to have been found suitable topic under research. The stage proves to be a turning point for the students aspiring to go for higher education. The highest and the lowest figures of the total drop-out in general over the period are 95.92% and 90.72 and against the figures of total tribal students of 95.37% and 84.80% respectively, that of tribal boys are 96.99% and 92.63% and girls, 98.38% and 95.43% respectively. This shows that as many as 3 to 7 Arunachalee boys and 2 to 5 girls out of every 100 are qualifying to go into higher education. Quite more alarming is the proportion of increase of drop-out of tribal girls compared to the tribal boys over the last 5 years. This trend seems to have been continuously repeated right from the primary to the higher secondary level which shows that the number of Arunachalee girls going for higher education is less than their counterpart boys. The number of Arunachalee students qualifying for higher education in the district ranges between 5 to 15 over the last quinquennial of 1994-95 to 1998-99, which appeared to be quite disheartening for the districts. This could be the central thing of the topic under investigation.

If we further go into the next stage of under-graduation the above figures are shown further getting low. Around 01 to 03 out of every 100 students both general and Arunachalee students qualify to go for university education.

It might be an imbalance proposition to harbour at a conclusion taking the figures in the undergraduation level because of the only Arts stream results of the government college, Bomdila over the period. But it could not be so much of an imbalanced one taking the admission issue of the students of three districts namely West Kameng, East Kameng and Tawang in only Arts stream into consideration. Though the students of science and commerce stream after passing out class XII are going out of the district for higher education whose number are not included in the figures shown still the number of students of Arts stream coming for admission to the only college of the district from the above mentioned three districts could be approximately the same with little variation with that of the number of students of science and commerce streams going out. Hence, basing upon the data available at the Government College, Bomdila the figure of drop-out shown in the above table cannot be completely illogical and hyperbolical.

The Table 5.9 reflecting the stage wise annual result of the district from 1990-91 to 1998-99 seems to have added cacophony to the above discussed alarming trend of drop-out rates.

The Table 5.9 shows the results of the secondary and higher secondary stage are very discouraging and discerning over the period. The lowest percentage of the results of class X is shown in 1995-96, i.e., 20.73 and the highest in 1993-94, i.e., 5016 against the average percentage of 38.0. At the higher secondary stage the average pass percentage is 40.79 with the lowest of 24.5% in 1992-93. These low average pass percentages both at secondary and higher secondary levels over the last eight years against 81.4% at primary and 75.39% at the middle levels (primary and middle stage results are not at least low) are going to badly affect the future educational perspectives of the district. In this context quite corroborative could be the fact

Table 5.9: Stagewise Annual Results of the District, w.e.f. 1990-91 to 1997-98

Year	*Class-V*			*Class-VIII*			*Class-X*			*Class-XII*			*+3 IIIrd Year*		
	No. of Candidates	No. of Candidates	Pass %	No. of Candidates	No. of Candidates	Pass %	No. of Candidates	No. of Candidates	Pass %	No. of Candidates	No. of Candidates	Pass %	No. of Candidates	No. of Candidates	Pass %
1990-91	641	505	78.78	303	240	79.20	266	128	48.12	146	96	65.75	9	5	55.55
1991-92	598	469	78.40	341	246	72.14	247	72	29.14	212	78	36.79	11	5	45.55
1992-93	601	486	80.96	325	213	65.53	325	128	39.38	156	38	24.35	12	8	66.66
1993-94	667	564	84.55	390	303	77.69	299	150	50.16	121	77	63.63	4	3	75.00
1994-95	704	660	93.75	449	403	89.75	226	108	47.78	111	52	46.84	11	9	81.81
1995-96	813	633	77.85	396	299	75.50	299	62	20.73	152	107	70.39	20	18	90.00
1996-97	788	627	79.56	450	326	72.44	387	133	34.36	101	55	54.45	33	24	72.72
1997-98	754	593	78.64	508	360	70.87	328	113	34.45	105	48	45.71	25	19	76.00
			Av.: 81.54			**Av: 75.39**			**Av.: 38.01**			**Av.: 40.79**			**Av.: 70.39**

Source: Field Study, Office of the DDSE, West Kameng District, Bomdila, Office of the Principal, Govt. College, Bomdila and District Statistical Handbooks.

that with higher percentage of failures of the students at secondary (around 62%) and at higher secondary (around 59%) levels the drop-out rates are bound to be burgeoning up. Hence, there is a need to thoroughly chalkout a state level plan to look into this gnawing problem and detail effective linings and systematically carry out them asking the arrest of the same.

6

THE PROBLEM AND THE CRITICAL EYE

Three types of questionnaires (Appendix I) have been prepared to study the objectives of the project, i.e. Basics of the dropouts. The Questionnaire I deals with the Family Background of a student dropped out which includes student's profile, educational history (class from which he dropped out), present status (whether employed or not), head of the household, parents' education, their income, his economic background, his access to modern facilities and his parents' response to modern facilities and to his wards' education.

In the Question No. 1, various heads like student's present village/town; village whether connected with pucca or kutcha roads, its distance from the district headquarters and circle office headquarters have been asked in order to gather information regarding the geographical situation of his village which certainly motivates a student whether or not to continue education under such circumstances.

Question dealing with the post-drop-out details of the student is an important one which entails student's justification to drop out. Student's parents' education, their income etc. have been asked to estimate family as well as moral support to the students being forced to drop out. The financial data of the family are felt needed to estimate the same. The question related to the student's as well his family's exposure to modern facilities is as important as the earlier ones to infer a valid analysis.

Some of the important issues related to the students dropping out as felt and experienced by the parents, have been given in order to testify his parents' attitude towards education as a whole and their wards' education specifically.

The Questionnaire II deals with twenty-four questions for the students who have dropped out which cover the student's interests in studies, school and in syllabus, his opinion about the teachers, friends, school co-curricular activities, principal-teacher relationship and above all, his attraction towards modern comfort goods and his desire to purchase them with no money etc.

From the Question No. 1, student's opinion of not continuing the education is reflected. It is asked about his teachers—their behaviour, their popularity, his favourite teacher etc. in order to examine his affinity towards the teaching community and teaching at large. Even he is asked about his school friends and curriculum in order to study his mentality towards his school during his studentship. Further the question aims at gradually wooing him towards being more forthcoming, frank and cooperative. Question No. 12 asking him about his school days seems to be an important one because here at, student's interests in school whether in studies or in stipends or in mid-day meals are shown. He is also enquired about his interests in other fields. The questions like the language the teachers uses in the class rooms and principal-teacher relationship have been asked to study the environment of class room teaching and the school which play a major role in motivating the students to regularly come to the school.

Some questions have been put to assess the student's personal interests towards society, his awareness towards modern luxurious goods and his desire to purchase them even if he does not have purchasing power during his studentship which naturally divert his attention from studies and subsequently motivate him to go for purchasing these goods as early as possible asking him to discontinue his schooling and earn money to materialise them. Further these questions go to relate to the demonstration effect to which young students as easy preys indiscriminately fall and subsequently drop out.

Questionnaire-III deals too with twenty-four questions for the teachers which include teacher's bio-data, his opinion about students, syllabus difficult subjects to be taught, method of teaching and necessary steps for better teaching standard, drop-outs, his respect in the society as a teacher, his problems; satisfaction with the infrastructure of the school available, shortcomings of the school, his insistence to the students as well as to parents not to encourage drop-outs and about Gaonburah. Another important purpose of this set of questions is to explore if the Gaonburah institution could be exploited to stabilise students' education in a given area on an extension of traditionally held grip that the Gaonburahs generally have over the daily pulse of the people in their individual jurisdictions.

Teacher's bio-data have been asked to draw a balance-sheet of his personal life and profession, his psychology and classroom environment, his career and his effort to strengthen his ability to teach etc. He is also questioned to seasonally answer on the characteristics of his students, their interests for coming to school and on main reasons of drop-outs that are intertwining to each other which form the basic structure of the topic under study. Teacher's happiness with his life, society's respect towards him, problems faced by him in his service career are some of the interesting questions put to him to decipher his orientation towards life, society and profession. Teacher's psychology of any sort is bound to be reflected in his class room teaching which ultimately moulds student's mentality whether or not to come to school. To perform his duty as a teacher, he is required to persuade the students and their parents not to encourage discontinuance of studies. This aspect has also been asked. A question on Gaonburah whether cooperative to the teaching community or not is there which definitely shapes a teacher's character in the remote areas to develop his inclination towards institutions and student's future.

Based on the data on the questionnaires collected by the scholar through his field survey of the different remote villages, circles and district headquarters the following tables have been devised and analysis and interpretations have been made to substantiate the objectives of the study. While the tables 6.1, 6.2, 6.3 and 6.4 have been derived from the Questionnaire No. 1, i.e. Family Based Questions; table 6.5 has been derived from the Questionnaires No. 2 (Students Based Questions), and the tables 6.6 and 6.7 from the Questionnaires No. 3, i.e. Teacher Based Questions.

Table 6.1: Persons Questioned

Different Categories of Respondants	*Strength*		
	Male	*Female*	*Total*
No. of students questioned	88	41	129
No. of parents/respondants questioned	82	47	129
No. of teachers questioned	82	25	107

What is evident from the above table is that most of the parents could be told all, belong to the poorer class, their educational background very low; 107 out of 129 (around 83%) are having no education at all, 17 of them have primary education, and only 5 of them middle level education. Even they lack accessibility to modern facilities. From the table it is clear that 42 out of 129 do not have any kind of modern facilities, whether it is radio, or television or newspaper, or Tape Recorder or watch or V.C.R. or V.C.P. The figure showing the accessibility to any one of facilities has burgeoned up to 87 out of 129 is due to the presence of either a radio or a watch in the family which is said to be

Table 6.2 Family Background of the Students Dropped-out

Income (In Rs.)	*Total No. of Respondents*	*Educational Qualifications*					*Occupation*		*Type of House*			*Access to Modern Facilties*
		Pry.	*Mid.*	*Sec.*	*Hr. Sec.*	*Nil*	*Agri-culture*	*Non-agri-culture*	*Owned*	*Rented*	*Any one*	*Nil*
1	*2*	*3*	*4*	*5*	*6*	*7*	*8*	*9*	*10*	*11*	*12*	*13*
0-5,000	113	12	3	–	–	99	102	–	87	–	19	42
5,000-10,000	16	5	2	–	–	8	24	3	28	14	68	–
Total	**129**	**17**	**5**	**–**	**–**	**107**	**126**	**3**	**115**	**14**	**87**	**42**

very inadequate to keep the parents as well as their school going wards up-to-date and well aware of the scenario happening outside.

Against such backdrop we can have a discussion on how much do schools and home background variables matter in the academic achievement of the students., Heyneman and Loxely (1982: 13-21 and 1983: 1162-94) of USA carried on a methodological study on the above issue and found that variations in school and teacher characteristics mattered little to student achievement, which was determined predominantly by home background. The only study in India which we find to have addressed this issue is Subrahmanyam's (1984). This examines the question of the relative influence of school and home on reading achievement with early 1980s data on 300 students in 15 primary schools in Andhra Pradesh. Using principal-component analysis it concludes that, in all, school factors account for 61% of total variation in achievement and home background factors explain 39%.

Why do Heyneman and Loxley's findings differ from that of the findings of Subrahmanyam could be discernible from the following observations. The student and family variables used in the statistical analysis of Subrahmanyam capture household socio-economic status and home educational environment more fully than Heyneman and Loxley data. In the latter's study, the background variables were pupils' age in months, sex and family's socio-economic status (SES) as proxied by some of the variables like mother's and father's education, father's occupation, number of books at home, and presence at home of a phonograph. The former's data have a much more extensive measure of family's economic status than Hayneman and Loxley measure. Moreover, the latter did not include many of the students personal characteristics which are highly important such as measure of ability, child's educational aspirations, whether student works to earn money, hours of home study per week, travel time to school and whether student takes private home tuitions.

Summing up, Geeta Gandhi Kindon (1998) opines that school quality and home background variables are related enough to make it difficult to statistically separate their two influences on achievement. Omission of school variables leads home background variables to pickup the former's influence and appear very significant. When school variables are added, the co-efficients and significance of background variable fall. Similar effects are observed if only school variables are regressed first and then background variables are included. There is no prime theoretical basis for dividing up the large common variance shared by home background and school quality.

Hence, parental variables like socio-economic status are highly correlated with cognitive development. Also the income ratio of the family is found to be predictive of the cognitive development of the child. Moreover, father's and mother's education is a dynamic factor directly related to cognitive development of the child encouraging long way for the smooth academic achievement.

Parental aspiration, parent-child interaction and dominance submission do not seem to show any definite relational trends in the scholar's study. Therefore, it is difficult to say with conviction how much part these variables play in the cognitive development of children. But since there seems to be a close connection between the general educational level of the home environment and the cognitive development of children, one may presume that educated parents will have better interaction with the child and will show a higher level of aspiration and at the same time, would be more democratic in their attitude. Children bring to the various socialisation settings in which they participate, various influences and aspects of their house and family backgrounds. Such family background factors, as its composition, socio-economic status, parental employment patterns and many others have been shown repeatedly to be related to children's responsiveness to schooling. The implication is obvious. This indicates the need to work with parents and to awaken general awareness in them.

Moreover, though the size of the class is not related with cognitive development, school fees and cognitive development are seen to be highly correlated. The amount of school fees and the socio-economic status of the parents go together. Most likely the higher SES group attends high fee charging school. Thus, schools may be effective not because they are high fee charging, but because they provide more and better facilities. Hence, greater the SES of the student, greater is his cognitive growth. The socio-economic status of parents, facilities for play, parental education, their expectations on child's education, the parent child interaction at home, child's nutritional level, self-concept, school fees, school facilities teacher's attitudes, school achievement, social distance and ethical discrimination are found to be highly correlated with the concept of all around academic development of the child in general and with the concept of number, length, area and volume in particular. This concept also shows significant relationship with the achievement test of arithmetic and language. And once a child lacks to have the above discussed both school and home background variables, he ceases to imbibe an interest in him to continue his education. He neither finds his school nor his home favourable encouraging and interesting to cultivate study. Swirling in skull-duggery he fails to decide whether to continue or drop education. Parental education and awareness play a major role in motivating the child at such a crossroad of his decision. If parents give null response the child given the condition chooses the simplest alternative of dropping out where he is not bothered about studies, home work, teachers' scolding and beating, annoyance at the question asked in the classroom and above all, the examination phobia; in a way he is set free.

His parents feel happy that without being perturbed about their children's education which inevitably would eat up much of their income, they are rather rendered freer about multiplying their family income with full-hearted participation of children in the earning process where no body around is to blame them for shifting students from schools to earning sites against the backdrop of children themselves bowing out from the schools. They thus stand naturally exonerated from the disgrace that is otherwise definite to issue from parents not exhibiting sufficient exemplary interest in their children's schooling. Easy and incontrovertible explanation on plea of their wards' failing and consequently opting out from the schools put forward by parents to cover up the actually pressing and gnawing financial hardships goes all the way to render the hapless and helpless children circumstantial wrecks whereas satisfied with the surface explanation the society and the government does not introduce any remedy to ameliorate such an innocuous-looking but socially largely hazardous malady. A saving grace, however, in the face of such an humbling reality would be that instead of either overlooking or partially glossing over the odd-inflicting ailment, the government and all others involved take a realistic look at the situation and do some such exercise that would ultimately not stigmatise the parents in the midst of their gruelling poverty as conniving is a socially handicapping cause in not giving their wards desirable level of education by way of providing them with financial capability to fund and finance their children's education.

Both the Tables 6.3 and 6.4 can be taken jointly for simultaneous analysis to arrive at a concrete conclusion of a fact. From the table 6.3 it is clear that most of the students drop out in between the age 10 to 15, the figure indicating 87 out of 129, a percentage of 67. A student within the age 10 to 15 mostly is coming within the classes V to X or roughly in between primary to secondary level

Table 6.3: Students' Educational Background

Age at the time of drop-out	**Years**		**Number and Percentage**
	1 to 10		22 (17)
	10 to 15		87 (67)
	15 and above		20 (16)
	Total		129 (100)
Total Years of Schooling	0 to 5		39 (30)
	5 to 8		63 (49)
	8 and above		27 (21)
	Total		129 (100)
Reason for dropping-out	Failure in Exams	P*	41 (32)
		S†	32 (25)
	Financial Problem	P	89 (69)
		S	112 (87)
	Health Problem	P	15 (12)
		S	31 (24)
	Problem related to school	P	Nil
		S	09 (07)
	Domestic Problem	P	34 (26)
		S	52 (40)
	Total	P	129
		S	129

*—Parents
†—Students
Note : Figures in the parentheses denote percentage.

Table 6.4: Parents' Awareness

Opinions of the Respondents	*Yes*	*No*	*Total*	*%age of Yes*
Goodness in going to School	114	15	129	88
Trying to send wards back to school	87	42	129	67
Obedience towards Parents	98	31	129	76
Happiness of wards in going to school	107	22	129	83
Value of Education in the Society	129	Nil	129	100

taking roughly the students entry into Class-1 at 5 which reflects that more number of students drop-out at these stages. That has exactly been corroborated in the next column, i.e. Total years of schooling. It is seen, 63 out of 129, around 49% have only 5 to 8 years of schooling, a high percentage in comparison to 30% having 0 to 5 years of schooling and 21% having 8 and above years of schooling. Even there is a very good response syndrome of the parents awareness what is reflected in the Table 6.4. Around 88% of the parents feel good the habit of their wards going to school regularly, 67% of them have tried to send their wards back to school even after dropped out, 83% have observed their wards happiness while going to school and more surprisingly 100% of the parents have realised the value of education in the society though 83% of them are completely illiterate (Table 6.2).

From the Table 6.4 it is also quite understandable that a good percentage of parents have tried to send their children to schools even after dropped out and as in the figure shown 76% of the parents have confessed the obedience of their wards towards them. Here the scholar is able to locate a contradiction in response to his analysis on the basis of Table 6.2 where parental initiatives to support their children's education have been discussed appalling and disheartening. But the figures in the Table 6.4 show a very good response from the parents' side so far their awareness to the sum totality of education is concerned. This contradiction or difference could be, as the scholar feels, due to the fact that a huge gap is felt created in between parents' awareness/ initiatives and their wards' carrying out of them. No doubt, the children obey their parents, their say what the parents opine according to the Table 6.4, but the way the children carry out their parents' say is not the way the parents think which remains unquestioned and unexplored for the parents. Hence, the figure of drop-outs over the years is getting quite alarming what is obvious from the previous chapter. What is implicit from it is that there does not have a symbiotic relationship between a student's family background or parental care or awareness or initiative or encouragement and his mentality to encash it outright. A happy coherence (honey mooning) is missing in between. Parents think they are performing their duties upto their satisfaction and the wards think they are just doing it by going to the school. For unnamed causes when the wards as school-goers only outwardly succeed in leech-like clinging to the inadequate family purse, they really come out from the school after a few years of schooling as helpless and useless drop-outs. Once a student is a school drop-out forever–he is a drop-out in the family, in the society and in the state as a whole. This is a ground where he feels himself completely insecured and is probably victimised by the anti-social, divisive and fissiparous elements like insurgency, terrorism, secessionism and communalism.

Children go to the school, it is good for the parents, they play and interact with their friends at home it is fine for the parents, they read at home, it is more encouraging for the parents in that the latter derive maximum motivational impetus from out of a kind of pathetic involvement in their own dream of straightening and defining the future of their children. 'Pathetic' because from what stands out from the observations posited above, the parents are left out in a lurch from where there is none to relieve them—illiteracy as a powerful hindrance on one hand disenables them from directly effectively interfering towards the whole mechanism, and on the other, the situational infrastructural lacuna in their multiplicity of varieties only helps aggravate the appallingness of the situation.

The reasons for drop-out have been shown in the Table 6.3 from which it is discernible that two different opinions have emerged, one from the student and the other from his parents/respondent, on various causes being responsible for the same. Financial problem, as the figures reflect, has claimed a larger percentage of drop-outs compared to the other kinds of factors, i.e. 87% (students' opinion) against 69% (Parents' opinion). While 40% of the students against a 26% of the parents have cited domestic problem as the reason for drop-outs, 32% of the former against a 25% of the latter have pointed out failure in the examination as the reason for the same. Further, this failure of the students on the examination as the parents taking decisions to neglect their wards' schooling is an interesting evidence that failure works just as a powerful alibi for parents justifying their disinterestedness in their wards' education one hand and using them in fields and other such apparently productive jobs by default. Problem related to health is shown to have claimed no less substantial a percentage (24% of students against 12% of parents corroborating the problem). One thing noticeable from the table in the column—reason for dropping-out is that excepting on one such reason, i.e. Failure in Examinations, on all other reasons the percentage of students' opinion is larger than that of percentage of their parents or respondents. Such figures seem to have come up due to the shifting or pushing up of responsibility deliberately from the students' side to that of the parents' to hide the former's loopholes, irresponsibility or carelessness contributing a potential denomination to the dynamics of the problem. Moreover, so far the issue of failure of examinations is concerned, lesser percentage of students' response has been observed corroborating the above connotation discussed. Rather students' responses hint at parents using their failure as a plea to mop up their poor economic background which works as a compelling deterrent to divert the children from the schools to other wage-earning sites to supplement family income.

We will get some supportive data with regard to the above discussion if we analyse the Table 6.5 derived from the questions put to the students during the present field survey at the different villages, circles, blocks and at the district headquarters.

Table 6.5: Students' Opinion About School and Environment

Sl. No.	*About*	*Opinions/Items*	*Number*	*Percentage*
1.	School	Very Good	36	28
		Good	87	67
		Bad	Nil	–
		Neither Good Nor Bad	6	5
2.	Teacher	Very Good	18	14
		Very Bad	Nil	–
		Neither Good Nor Bad	111	86
		Extremely Bad	Nil	–
3.	Having Friendship	Yes	129	100
		No	Nil	–
4.	Toughness of Curriculum	Yes	57	44
		No	72	56
5.	Teacher-H.M./Principal Relationship	Good	92	71
		Bad	18	14
		Average	–	–
		Extremely Good	6	5
		Unanswered	13	10
6.	Extra-Curricular Activities	Games	56	43
		Cultural	62	48
		Literary	7	5
		Nil	39	30
7.	Influenced by	Rich	18	14
		Educated	53	41
		Powerful	7	5
		Salaried	61	47
8.	Attraction Towards	Crowd	122	87
		Garments	73	57
		Cosmetics	61	47
		Automobiles	67	52
		Palatable Dishes	109	84
		Electronic Goods	122	95
		Tambola/Dice	106	82
		Others	–	–

9.	Desire to Purchase Without Money	Garments	89	69
		Cosmetics	61	47
		Vehicles	123	95
		Palatable Dishes	109	84
		Electronic Goods	122	95
10.	Difficult Subjects	Maths.	129	100
		English	121	93
		Others	—	—
11.	Friends Belonging to	Same Locality	118	91
		Same Caste	113	88

The figure shown in the above table on various subjects correspond positively to our previous discussion about school and home background variables. Around 67% of the students interviewed told their school to be good, 86% were indifferent, 100% had the friends during their schooling, 71% felt the teacher-principal relationship good, more percentage of students (56%) seemed to have found the curriculum not tougher and moreover, a good number of students confessed to have participated actively in extra curricular activities, i.e.—48% in cultural and 43% in sports and games activities. Quite disheartening has been the figure reflecting the percentage of students participated in literary activities (5% only). Ninety-five per cent of students (122 out of 129) during their schooling found literary items to be a distant field of interest. The scholar tried his level best during his field-survey to find out the cause of their least participation in literary activities. The students expressed themselves weak at English both in writing and speaking which might be a corroborated cause of the problem discussed above or might be due to the first generation education. Moreover, the figures and percentages available with us on extra-curricular activities are very discouraging compared to the same on other areas.

So far students' opinion on their schools, teachers, teacher-principal relationship, friends and curriculum are concerned, we get a very clear understanding of the fact that the students had been mustered and nourished under a good and healthy school administration and surroundings and equipped with sound school variables. Hence, it is presumed that home background or other kinds of variables would have worked against the students' discontinuance of studies. This point could be clear if we further analyse the other columns of the table 6.5. It has been observed that most of the students during their studentship have not been restrained or controlled by their inordinate passions. More than 80% of them have been attracted by material objects like crow, palatable dishes, electronic goods and the gambling game of dice or tambola whenever they were coming across them in cities or towns. Even a good number of them has been attracted towards costly garments, fancy cosmetics and various kinds of vehicles. Many of them have opined that they had the desire to purchase those goods which had attracted and allured them during their student career even if they did not have the purchasing power. The percentage shown in the table in this connections seems to have been high—69% in respect of cosmetics (mostly girls), 95% of vehicles, 84% of palatable dishes and 95% in respect of electronic goods. This kind of phenomenon suggests that students get mostly pre-occupied with the material aims and desires during their studenthood which inspire and instigate them to go for procuring their material objectives at an early age. This further encourages them to earn money as early as possible to cherish their desires which ultimately sees in them a kind of disinterest asking them to go for drop-out and embracing other means to earn money.

To aggravate their materialistic desire and the desire to drop-out, their disinterest towards Mathematics and English amounting to an insurmountable psychological burden acts almost like a camouflaging agent asking them to move away from a restricting world of studies that is endlessly attended by a hoard of anuseating and phobia-building factors.

Let us now switch over to two other tables 6.6 and 6.7 which have been derived from the questionnaires put to the teachers of various educational institutions starting from primary to higher secondary. Table 6.6 shows the teachers' profile-their age, educational qualifications, training their average weekly hours spent in taking classes, in doing official duties and in personal work etc. Teachers' average family members, i.e. 4. Detail discussion on teachers' qualifications, their training accommodation etc. of the district has been made in the previous chapter.

From the Table 6.7 showing the teachers's response it can be presumed that the teachers, despite their problems and odds, have put up a sincere effort towards their profession. As large as 78% of teachers have cited inadequate medical facilities as their main problem, 67% have cited that of accommodation and 43% that of frequent transfer. All such problems are bound to affect one teacher in his class room environment and teaching.

Moreover, the scholar during his field study has realised another grievous problem in the village areas, i.e. the posting of one teachers in a primary school (47 out of 98, around 48%, see Table 5.6a in the previous chapter). Taking all classes from class I to V and teaching all subjects right from Basic Science to English lying in between Social Studies, Mathematics and Hindi etc. in a limited span of school time seem to be hyperbolic and illogical as it requires of single teachers an unreasonable amount of energy and patience if a commitment to the profession works behind keeping him constantly inspired. It is not simply humanly possible to engage such different streamlined oriented classes within an almost impossible period of time. Hence, on all such contest the primary education is bound to be adversely affected. Even students find it disinterested and disgusting to be taught by a single teacher on all subjects. The trend of one teacher-teaching if continues for a long time, compels students to think negative and encourages them not to come

Table 6.6 Teacher's Profile

Age (No.)			Educational Qualifications			Nos. Having Special Training	Average Pay Monthly	Average Members To Be Supported	Accomodation		Average Weekly Working Hours		
Less than 30 Years	30 to 45 Years	45 to 60 Years	Interme-diate & Lower Class	Graduate	P.G. & Above				Kutcha	Pucca	In Class	In Official Duties	In Personal Work
1	2	3	4	5	6	7	8	9	10	11	12	13	14
33	49	25	36 (34%)	39 (36%)	32 (30%)	62 (58%)	Rs. 8285.00 (apprx.)	04	49 (46%)	58 (54%)	18	03	12

Table 6.7 Teacher's Response

Sl. No.	*Aspects*	*Opinions*	*No. of Teachers*	*%age (Apprx.)*
1	*2*	*3*	*4*	*5*
1.	Problems	Frequent Transfer	46	43
		Accomodation	72	67
		Medical	83	78
		Others	55	51
2.	Reasons for drop-outs	Failure in Exams.	61	57
		Financial	92	86
		Health	38	36
		Problems related to school	33	31
		Domestic	74	69
		Others	–	–
3.	Behaviour of Goanburah	Very cooperative	11	10
		Non-cooperative	–	–
		Indifferent	–	–
		Average	96	90
4.	Happiness with life	Yes	78	73
		No	27	25
5.	Social respect	Yes	89	83
		No	16	15
6.	Insistence not to drop-out	To parents (Yes)	62	58
		To students	77	72
		To parents (No)	43	50
		To students	28	26
7.	Improvement in teaching	Yes	91	85
		No	14	13
		Audio-visual	56	52
		Training	69	64
		Others	46	43
8.	Nature of syllabus	Tough	–	–
		Easy	–	–
		Alright	107	100
9.	Infrastructure	Sufficient	16	15
		Insufficient	91	85

10.	Insufficiency in infrastructure	Lack of class rooms	60	56
		Lack of laboratory	42	39
		Lack of library	73	68
		Lack of playground	66	62
		Lack of furniture	81	76
		Lack of accomodation	63	59
		Lack of hostel	72	67
		Others	–	–

to the school. They find it discouraging and boring to see the same face teaching, all subjects, tougher and easier, English to Mathematics without any kind of noticeable changes in his tonal and facial expression. Once a student stops coming to school, the frequency increases which leads to a situation where he finds himself emotionally deranged, physically stressed and mentally and psychologically perturbed to continue his education.

The table also reflects good figures regarding teachers' respect in the society and their happiness towards life. Around 73% of the teachers have expressed their happiness towards life, 83% of them have claimed to have enjoyed societal prestige and dignity as teachers even if they have been haunted by a series of problems discussed above. One thing which looks transparent from the opinion of the teachers is that the growth of the problem of drop-out cannot be ascribed to a single variable. There could be the multiplicity of variables and factors contributing to the cause of it. If we just look at the serial no. 8 i.e. the nature of the syllabus, we find 100% of teachers have said the syllabi for all classes to be alright according to the age group of the children. This suggests that the children are not at all incredibly exposed to the higher quality study materials which go beyond their mental horizon to cope up. Rather they are systematically and psychologically trained to the nature and dynamics of the study materials from the lower class as per their grasping capacity. Hence, the nature of the syllabus could not be considered to be tougher to be at all a causation for the problem of drop-out. Mention may be made here of our finding with reference to Table No. 6.5 where students find Mathematics and English to be highly taxing. Teachers' assessment of the situation, thus, is at odds if students' honest forthrightness regarding their grey encounters is taken into a sympathetic considerations. At a time when we are moving towards a learner-centered approach in education this imbalance in students' vs. teachers' evaluation of the existing syllabus will have to be seriously reviewed if any thing concrete is to be delivered.

Of course, the teachers in large number have cited the problems related to school environment to be very discouraging. Even they have demanded more and more improvement in teaching ethics. Around 85% of them (SI No. 7) have stressed upon the need of improving the mechanism of teaching—64% of them have asked for their in service training from time to time in order to update their teaching skill so as to make the classroom environment more interesting as well as the system of fee-back more effective; 52% have called for the audio-visual aids and 43% for other kinds of aids basically stressing upon computer linked education like Computer Assisted Instruction (CAI) and Computer Aided Learning), both barely necessary for effective classroom teaching. So fare as the audio-visual aids are concerned, television happens to be an important organ. Television technology permits transmission of live programmes or motion pictures by cable, microwave, instructional, fixed stationery items, satellite or conventional broadcasting to schools or colleges or other institutions to view instructional programmes live or to record them for subsequent use. Local production of instructional units is also possible that are not available from any other source. Students benefit from a variety of materials of educational value derived from programmes that they view at home.

More purposively, education television could be utilised dealing with programmes which primarily educate rather than entertain. The schools should provide effective viewing conditions and it is the responsibility of the teachers to make use of educational television to the maximum possible extent. Even the students must be involved in follow-up activities soon after a particular programme is displayed.

Mention may be made here that the success of education through television involves careful planning. Training of teachers is essential to make the best use of the equipment and programmes telecast. The centre for educational technology of the NCERT has launched such training programmes with the help of resource persons drawn from primary level to secondary teacher education. A manual has been developed and translated into various regional languages. Pupils exposed to educational television are found to perform better in achievement tests than others. But for best results a careful planning in instructing the T.V. syllabus in relation to classroom and orientation of teachers to make best use of the medium needed. The NCERT has produced educational television programmes for its telecast, for example, INSAT-IB was intended in the morning hours. Direct Reception Sets (DRS) and VHF sets receive the programmes relayed by grand stations and relay centres. The NCERT has set up a Central Institute for Education Technology (CIET) merging its Centre for Educational Technology (CET) and Department of Teaching Aids for all such programmes. Along with the suggestions for improvement of teaching skill, the teacher have pointed out the handicapping of the school environment. Around 85% of them have cited respective school infrastructure inadequate—56% have found this inadequacy in the availability of classrooms, 39% of laboratory, 68% of library facilities, 62% of playground, 76% of furniture, 59% of teachers' accommodation, and above all, 67% of hostel facilities for both boys and girls. The schools of the district with such magnitude of infrastructural inadequacy in the areas discussed above, are bound to be handicapped to produce sound educational atmosphere. Even in some areas of the district the teachers have expressed their inability to get their doubt cleared before going for class-teaching due to shortage of library facilities and good quality reference books. This happens to be the worst part of the dynamics of teaching and the teacher hides that information from passing on to students on which his doubts have not been cleared. Once subject related informations are left unpassed, students remain unaware of the greater connotation of the topic discussed. Hence, the classroom teaching as a whole loses its own solidarity. The whole system gets haphazard pleasing neither the teacher nor the students of the class-room. Students generally develop a wrong impression on that teacher and as a result, avoid his classes. Moreover, they also develop distaste towards that particular subject in which they find their teachers adequately confused. The whole process this way, serves as a stepping-stone to the mechanism of drop-outs and failures. This holds a convincing plea to explain our finding in Table 6.5, Serial No. 2 citing students' general lack of concrete appreciation of teacher quality which basically has to issue out from the quality of classroom teaching—as high as 86% of the students have exhibited disturbing indifference on the quality assessment of the teachers.

The bottleneck posing a threat to the spread of higher education in the district and strangulating the fate of the district has been the problem of the drop-outs. Teachers do positively corroborate to this malady. Even they have also tried to check this problem through awareness and creating consciousness among the parents and their children who have dropped out. From the table 6.7 (Serial No. 6) it can be observed that 58% of teachers have opined to have persuaded the parents to send their wards to the school even they ahve dropped out and 72% of them have indicated to have motivated the students to resume their studies in the school. The response to their insistence to both the parents and their wards has been reported to be very slow and negligible. The teachers have also held the view that some students, after their insistence and to some extent pressurized by their parents, do turn up to the school, maintain regularity for a week or two or for a maximum period of one month and once again choose to drop-out. Moreover, the parents when asked about the result of the teachers' insistence on them to motivate their wards not to drop-out have expressed their helplessness about improving their wards regular attendance pattern in the school while in principle agreeing to the very need of their positively interfering to help arrest the drop-out menace.

The teachers when asked about the reasons for dropouts have come up with numerous explanations. While around 57% of them refer to the failure in examinations as a reason 86% refer to the financial problems, 36% to the health problem of the students, 31% to the problems related to school and 69% refer to their domestic problem. Mention may be made here that the domestic problem is a synthesised form of the many hydra-headed family-tradition custom-bound tensions and obligations by which the students during their student career get victimised, lose their seredipity in the dungeon of aimless life and become wayward.

The problem includes early marriage of the students (basically in the Secondary School level); early parenthood without realising respectively (practically in equipped to realise at such a tender age) the imminent gnawing repercussion on attaining parenthood too early; the presence of no earning member in the family to give sustenance which a student/child cannot corporally avoid being an ageing, adolescent and dependable member of the family; helping the parents in the cultivation and agricultural production at a time when the school syllabus is covered fast; looking after the young brothers and sisters when parents are away on the agricultural fields absenting from the school; and above all, putting their labour outside for hours for the sake of money to feed their needy family members a situation they could not but realise to do so etc. The effect of such kind of adolescent employment asking the students to discontinue education could be well understood from the following discussions.

Studies have found that over half the 10th graders and nearly all the 11th and 12th graders work sometime during the school year (Manning: 1990). The National Commissions and groups have advocated a greater link between high school and adolescent employment, as have researchers of adolescent society such as Coleman (1961), who have espoused the establishment of a closer connection between the major domains of adolescence, including school and work. The increased emphasis on adolescent employment has even become prominent in the popular culture, with studies indicating parental support for adolescent employment (Phillips and Sandstorm: 1990).

Adolescent employment is not universally accepted as being a positive experience, however. Although some empirical studies (such as Greenberger and Steinberg: 1986; Lewin-Epstein: 1981) have indicated that it is positively related to increased academic achievement, commitment, and self-esteem, others have concluded that it may actually have detrimental consequences for teenagers. Specifically, researchers have contended that employment may pull students out of high school or higher secondary school prior to graduation for a variety of reasons (Bickel and Milton: 1983; Papagiannis, Bickel and Fuller: 1983), including their desire to obtain the status of adult roles and their lack of integration into the school environment resulting from excessive employment. If this is the case, although adolescent employment may give students work experience and potentially valuable job skills, it may also greatly decrease their later attainment levels and life chances by increasing the likelihood of their dropping out of high school. Although research on the various individual attributes associated with dropping out of high school has been extensive, few studies have empirically examined the relationship between adolescent employment and dropping out.

Given the complexities of today's employment possibilities for adolescents, examining the relationship between work and dropping out should encompass more than just employment intensity. The jobs held by today's youths are drastically different from those in years past, and the attributes of these jobs vary, depending on the work setting and environment (Greenberger and Steinberg: 1986). For example, work in a food service occupation is of a different nature than that performed in a retail store or factory; these occupations and sectors vary in a number of different ways, including the chance to apply classroom based knowledge, amount of direct supervision, income, ability to apply higher-order thinking skills, and oppor-tunities for future employment.

Because of these intraoccupational differences, type of employment may have an independent effect on dropping out, net of individual students' attributes and hours of employment. Furthermore, findings between the intensity of employment and dropping out may be clarified if the relationship between hours worked and dropping out varies according to the type of job; for example, working in a higher-paying, higher-skill industry (manufacturing or technical) may cause the relationship between hours worked and dropping out to be intensified compared to the same relationship for students who are employed in the service sector.

Not that demographic characteristics contribute predominantly for the school drop-outs, but many other forces may push or pull students out of school. One possibility is that students are pulled out of school or rationally choose work over school. For example, students who are most likely to drop out (such as poor minority students) may leave not because of a disjuncture between their aspirations and expectations, but because they freely choose to do so for more promising prospects like employment.

In fact, labour markets pull students out of school when there is a greater demand for low-skill, low-paid labour (Duncan: 1965) or when the unemployment rate is exceptionally low. Moreover, dropouts rationally choose work over school for many competing reasons (Bickel and Milton: 1983), including a desire to obtain the status of adult roles. For example, some of the drop-outs when asked by the scholar indicated that they left schools because they either wanted or felt they needed to work. D'Amico (1984) found that students who work more than 20 hours a week are less likely to drop out and those who work fewer than 20 hours a week are less likely to drop out than are students who do not work at all. He contended that students who work in excess of 20 hours per week have less time and energy to devote to academics and are thus more likely to drop out. In contrast, students who work fewer than 20 hours per week learn key traits, such as persistence and dependability, that carry over into their schooling—making them less likely to drop out.

Barro (1984) has given a different kind of opinion on this pattern between hours worked and dropping out. He stated that working fewer than 15 hours per week has little effect on students dropping out. However, he noted that students who work 15-21 hours per week have 50 percent higher drop-out rates and those who work more than 21 hours per week have 100 percent higher drop-out rates than do those who work 0-14 hours per week. In contrast, McNeal (1995) found a curvilinear relationship between hours worked and dropping out, which suggests that minimal employment is beneficial and excessive employment is detrimental to students remaining in high school. Specifically, he indicted that students who work more than 7 hours per week have a significantly higher likelihood of dropping out.

Many factors may contribute to this myriad of seemingly contradictory findings. First, there may be no clear relationship between the intensity of employment and dropping out.

Second, this range of findings may be an artifact of the different operationalisations for hours used in each study and thus may mask the actual relationship.

Third, there may be significant variation in the relationship between intensity of employment and dropping out (either in functional form or magnitude) that is masked by lumping all occupational categories into a single analysis. For example, excessive employment may be more detrimental for students' retention when it is undertaken in a high-skill-high-paying occupation than in alow-skill-low paying occupation; that is, there may be more of a pulling-out effect when a student is employed in an occupation or industry in which he or she perceived an opportunity for immediate and substantial employment.

Fourth, there may be significant gender variation in the relationship between hours worked and dropping out that also masks the actual relationship between hours worked and dropping out coupled with samples of different compositions, could yield seemingly different and contradictory results.

Thus, the urgent need of the hour is to significantly change how sociologists of education, educators, policy makers, and parents think about the children's education and employment. There should be an organic resolution in their thought motivating the global perspectives of education and mooting out a trend to help arrest the dangerous growth of the dropout percentage at all stages of general education catering to the both societal and individual needs.

All sorts of variables-whether school, domestic or societal-pushing the healthy educational surroundings to a morbid anatomy of horrible vicissitudes precipitating a lineage of dropout and above all, putting the entire process of the state on the likelihood of students dropping out is reason for concern. Policy makers have long contended that one way to socialise teenagers to become young adults is to encourage them to work. However, these findings indicate that there is a negative, unintended consequence of adolescent employment: a higher likelihood of dropping out.

Intensity of employment leading to an increased likelihood of dropping out is also a concern for sociological research. Social control and integration theories traditionally contend that the more integrated individuals are into society, the less likely they are to commit deviant acts. It is conceivable that adolescent employment can be conceptualized as a proxy for some form of integration, either into the world of work or the community. If this is the case, then the problem of dropout which is definitely a deviant act could be arrested if creative forms of education are introduced so that greater levels of integration of the societal kind could be ensured. This finding indicates the need to conceptualise more fully the roles of various institutions in forming behaviour. For example, although work is traditionally seen as a normative structure that contributes to the socialisation of adolescents, it may also foster negative habits and attitudes that sever students' ties to schooling.

Researchers, educators and policy makers must realise that adolescents are employed in diverse occupational arenas and bring various individual attributes to the workplace. These two factors work in tandem to produce a wide range of effects on students' outcomes—a complexity that future research and policy initiatives must account for more fully. To overlook such subtle variation may well lead to the false conclusion that involvement in some behaviour, such as adolescent employment, has a positive effect on students' involved contribution to the purpose of schooling, rather than that the benefits and/or detriments of the behaviour are contingent on a wealth of criteria.

7

EPILOGUE

The closing decade of the second millennium has witnessed far-reaching political, economic and technological development that have affected life styles and practices all over the world. The breakdown of political barriers, spread of free market economy and a knowledge explosion following exceptional developments in communication technology have contributed to the ushering in of an era of globalisation. This phenomenon, often described as spacetime compression, promises to have dynamic implications on higher education the world over. In the fifty years since Independence the Indian higher education system has undergone a unique transformation from an elitist to an egalitarian one as a result of the impact of the two paradigm shifts of the western world, i.e. replacement of selective learning over a period of time to a life-long learning for all and the teacher-centered model to learner-centered model. India barely needs the fuller implementation of these changed ideas. In the Article 45 of the Indian Constitution, the commitment of the newly independent nation to provide universal education was enshrined. The task was taken up with earnestness by the state and there has been a phenomenal expansion of education system in past fifty years. But the challenge of providing universal elementary education (UEE) became increasingly difficult to achieve because gains of the expansion of the school system continued to get offset by the high population growth. The goal of achieving universal literacy receded faster than the effort put in to catch up with it. After forty years of

Independence there were more illiterates than the total population of the country at the time of independence. According to the census of 1991, out of every 1000 men 641 and out of every 1000 women 392 could read and write.

The quantitative expansion of the school system in the independent India continued to follow the model of the primary school education introduced by the colonial government. It was a costly model because it involved construction of school buildings, appointment of teachers and expansion of the bureaucratic students for the management of the state's school system. Invariably, new schools were opened up without ensuring the essential learning conditions. Shortcuts such as starting rural primary schools with only one classroom and appointing one teacher when at least two were required seem to have been indiscriminately followed. Often untrained teachers who did not possess the prescribed levels of education were appointed. It is, therefore, not surprising that researches have also revealed that the post-independence expansion of the school system has entailed dilution of the quality of education. Also, there have been few serious efforts to evolve cost effective indigenous models of school education relevant to the needs of the people of our country. The end result is that even after 50 years of independence, the colonial legacy of an impersonal school system, marked mainly by its utility as a passport for employment and for upward social mobility, continues as the driving force for running it.

According to the Registrar General of India (1997), the projected child population in the age group 6-14 years in 1996 was 187,704,000. In the academic year 1996-1997 the estimated number of children enrolled in the primary stage (classes 1 to 5) was 110.4 million and the estimated number of children enrolled in the upper primary stage (classes 6 to 8) was 41.0 million. Therefore, about 36.3 million children of this age group were out of school. For taking care of education on the out-of-school children at the rate of one teacher for forty children 9.07 lakh new teachers will be required.

According to the Sixth All India Educational Survey (AIES 1998) recently conducted by the NCERT the total number of teachers in position in the primary and upper primary schools were 20.13 lakh and 10.36 lakh respectively whereas for educating 151.4 million children at the rate of one teacher for 40 children 37.85 lakh teachers should have been in position. Therefore, additional 7.35 lakh teachers may have to be appointed in the primary and upper primary schools if the teacher-pupil ratio is to be maintained at 1:40. The annual salary of an elementary school teachers including allowances at the entry level of the Fifth Pay Commission pay scales is Rs. 85,680. Therefore, the recurring financial burden on the state for meeting the salary component of the new teachers will be Rs.14,068 crore.

In addition to appointment of teachers new class rooms will have to be built in school. Their number can also be estimated. If for each group of 40 children one classroom is to be made available then the number of classrooms required for 187.7 million children will be 46.91 lakh. The total number of class rooms in the primary and the upper primary schools as per the 6th AIES are 21,29,300. Therefore, 25,63,300 additional classrooms may have to be built in the schools. If a modest provision of rupees one lakh for constructing one class room is made the no-recurring financial liability on the state under this head will be Rs. 25,633 crore. Over and above, these estimated funds will be required for the training of new teachers and for providing mid-day meal, books and uniforms for children. Funds of this magnitude are not available with the state. Therefore, the commitment of the state to provide free and compulsory education to all children in the age group of 6 to 14 years has been reduced to a pipe dream.

Because of the financial constraints it has not been possible for this state to improve the infrastructure in its schools and the essential learning conditions have seldom been met. This has resulted in lack of confidence in the ability of state's schools to provide quality education. Even those parents who can ill afford to meet the cost of education of their children prefer to struggle and avail of education in private schools for their children. It should, therefore, not shock us when we find that high fee charging private schools have mushroomed even in the rural areas. The worst affected are the children belonging to the tribal groups and those belonging to the scheduled castes. What is the way out of the prevailing impasse? The way out is to liberate education from the dictates of the Western thought and to adopt an indigenous model of education based on the thoughts of thinkers like Gandhi, Sri Aurobindo, Tagore, Swami Dayanand, Vivekanand and many others who toady are silently carrying out experiments on education relevant to the ethos of our country. Cost effective models of education are to be evolved for providing contextual and relevant education for meeting the varying geographical and social conditions.

Among the states of India, Arunachal Pradesh is comparatively young as it attained full statehood only in 1987. The state still strives to make full use of its potential and to progress rapidly towards development despite it being known as an excluded area just a few decades ago. Like many other states Arunachal has not been an exception to the substantial demands on educational management and administration. Even if, the state government has made concerted efforts, particularly during the eighties, to improve various aspects of education and its management, there are still several perspectives which need special attention, including some of the major educational tasks with particular reference to future prospects along different dimensions of education. It is considered to be one of the backward states of the country with reference to its literacy percentage which is only 41% as per 1991 census as against 52% for all India, its female literacy being only 29 per cent. Even its neighbouring north-eastern states like Assam, Manipur, Mizoram, Meghalaya and Tripura have higher percentages of literacy—both female as well as overall. Assam has a literacy rate of 53% with female literacy of 43%, Manipur 61% with female literacy of 49%, Meghalaya 48% with female literacy 45%, Mizoram 81% with female literacy of 78% and Tripura 60% with female literacy of 50%. Arunachal Pradesh has therefore to struggle hard to raise its literacy levels.

It is true that for all these years, the tribals of the state had shown an apathy towards literacy and education, but the situation seems to be improving. The villages have started showing interest in education, and the Panchayat Raj Institutions are coming forward to help in this essential task. Like several other states of India have taken up projects by selecting some districts for the purpose of achieving total literacy through mass campaign and involvement of local people and other agencies, some serious efforts need to be made by the state to make some of its thirteen districts totally literate in a given span of time through mass campaign and involvement of teachers, students, voluntary agencies, employers, mass media, etc. with a special attention to promote female literacy.

The district West Kameng with a total population 56,421 as per 1991 census, 7th in the order of total population the districts in the state, has got 36.48% of literacy, 2nd in the literacy rate among the districts. So far the male and female literacy rates in the state are concerned, West Kameng occupies third position reflecting the percentages of 44.72 and 27.06 respectively. Moreover, the district's decennial growth rate of population (1981-1991) seems to be encouraging, i.e., 35.74 falling below the state's growth rate of 35.86. Against such literacy data of the district, special attention needs to be emphasised for the development of higher education. Though the district has got a degree college at its headquarters catering to the demands of the three districts, West Kameng, East Kameng and Tawang, it enrols very less number of students a year and too sends very less number for further higher education.

The objectives of the topic were to find out the possible reasons checking the growth of higher education in the district. To reach at a logical conclusion on the issue discussed above, the scholar made wide survey in various circles of the district, interviewed drop-outs, their parents or guardians and teachers, collected data from various sources, analysed them and finally reached to the following conclusions.

Findings

- The initiative from the side of the government has been phenomenal with regard to the expansion of education in general with distant corners also having been covered under the educational plan.

  (i) An overall increase by 35% in the growth of the institutions has been recorded in the district of West Kameng alone over a decade period from 1989-90 to 1998-99.

  (ii) Pre-primary schools have recorded an increase of 21%; primary schools 34%; the middle schools 62% and the secondary schools 17%.

  (iii) On the side of the higher education not withstanding the low enrolment potential and still lower inclination among students for general stream education as approved to technical education, higher secondaries have multiplied by an astounding 150% and a college for the Arts students has been opened even though establishment of a college entails a very high cost.

(iv) The teacher pupil ratio at the school level is very satisfactory as it is far higher than the national average (1:20 in place of 1:30).

(v) A strong potential already exists to render the district a lead district in terms of quality education though existing form of educational administration in the district has to be thoroughly overhauled to make it more responsive towards the fast changing nature of the growing demands for education in various corners of the district.

- Teachers education being undeniably an anchor and determinant of the quality of education everywhere the state in pursuit of its hurried teacher recruitment plan has not given adequate attention to recruit trained teachers to desired level (Only 24.36% of the teachers so far are trained—8.46% at primary, 10.75% at middle, 24.35% at secondary and 62.5% at the higher secondary levels.)

- The potential for quality education spotted above is countered due to the untrained opulence of teachers on one hand and poor teacher accommodation facilities at the school sites on the other. Further compounding of the problem issues out of the poor hostel provisions for the students. Drop-out of the girls especially is essentially born out of this singular lack of hostel provision. Only a meagre 17.04% schools have got hostels; 29.06% HT, ILC, LT, MIBT and OBT school rooms paint the gloomy scene of the poor infrastructural strength of the schools which appears to be working very strongly to encourage increase of the dropout problem at the school level.

- In comparison to the total drop-out rate recorded for the study period, the tribal students exhibit a higher dropping out tendency.

(i) At primary level fluctuation for tribal students being within 58.61% to 65.45% as against the total drop out rate fluctuating within 50.95% to 60.69%.

(ii) At middle school level the total drop-out rates fluctuations between 70.87% and 83.03% whereas the tribal students make up the figure from 75.39% to 84.64%.

(iii) The tribal girls dropping out account for 85.88% in comparison to the tribal boys for 83.66%.

(iv) The tribal students drop-out to the extent between 95.37% and 84.80% with the girls outnumbering the boys.

(v) By the time entry into higher education is considered only 3 to 7 out of every 100 tribal boys and 2 to 5 out of every 100 tribal girls are seen entering into the undergraduate level of education.

(vi) The 95% in case of boys and about 98% in case of girls are quite serious figures of drop-out which urgently require to be effectively addressed to if the district in particular and consequently the state in general are to register any recognizable progress in terms of higher education worth the name.

- About the quality of education to make any statement exclusively basing on the school terminal examinations is of not much use since the question of quality education at the school level despite conductive factors operating such as appreciable teacher student ratio is offset due to other negative factors like poor infrastructural facilities etc. working more strongly to counter the prospects of gains from the existing potentialities.
- Under the present scheme of things it is found that through adequate government initiative schools of various levels have been provided well within the reach of the students of various age groups. Accordingly

primary schools come first in priority and hence the highest number of the primary schools in the district. Gradual upward arrangements could be distinctly reasonably seen to be reducing in number to justify the feeding strength of students from a convenient clubbing of villages. Even though drop-out problem due to a host of other salient factors assumes a very disturbing proportion government does not appear to be exclusively held responsible since in its planning of providing schools at least at the present level of concern and consideration, it still appears to convincingly playing a serious and sincere role though on other management fronts responsibility could be definitely fixed with it

- Parental education is at an abysmally low level in the district which acts as a very powerfully determining factor that is helplessly in a sorry state of inaction when intervention of any reasonable effective sort is demanded from them. A complicated handicapping poor socio-economic condition almost amorphous in its disturbing presence accounts for further diluting the intervening potential of the parents. It can be seen that the poor ignorant parents are at a losing end since both when they do not know how their wards' education could help them in their later advanced years and when they know of the sure gains promised by education, they fail either to activate their wards for schooling or to retain them in the schools till the completion of the scheduled school years. The Adult Education given in the recent years appears to have contributed to growth of awareness of the parents about the benefictions of the education and parents have been rendered able in a limited way to contribute positively towards their wards' schooling.

- Parents, perpetual preoccupation with the problem of daily bread many times compels them either to act as passive on lookness to the spectacle of their wards dropping out in the mid-course of their schooling when the wards coming out of the schools at their pleasure add to the family income in whatever meagre way possible.

(i) More often than not drop-outs from schools are found to be busy in many wayward activities without caring much for supplementing the family income by gainfully supporting their parents in their daily wage-earning business.

(ii) Some exposure to the world governed by a consumerist culture earned during schooling period generates in the students an avid interest for individual possession of many new things. To procure these things many times it is reported that the drop-outs turned new earners in the family set aside their own income while at times also demanding or even stealing a part of the parents' income. Thus, it can be seen that after dropping out, children in a family instead of that gleefully turning out into naturally assets for their parents from point of view of additional potential for income, become unfore thought of liabilities. The misery of the poor and helpless parent is increased when drop-outs in a family first appear. This is mostly the case with the post-middle school drop-outs or the drop-outs from the primary schools with an unreasonable late start.

- During the field study the scholar has been led to think that in the high figure of parental illiteracy is submerged the higher and more frequent incidence of mother's illiteracy which accounts for the absence of a loving, caring and effectively persuasive influence within the family framework which fails to put back the drop-outs into the schools. Interviews have pointed out that mother's attendance in the Adult Education Centres is almost next to inial. Thus, when semi-aware fathers in the families somehow feel concerned about their wards' education, the mothers in absence of any such inspiring and motivating futuristic vision sometimes contribute to a clash of parental perspectives whereunder family's instant and emergency needs loom to be of greater significance and under a unsupportive emotional climate, prospects of wards' schooling lie marred.

- The scholar is further driven to ponder over the problem of parental perspectives which owe their origin and derive their continued sustenance from the appalling poverty that hardly allows for any thought beyond that of the daily bread. A cool family emotional atmosphere that is always a natural attendant of a minimum reasonable level of income in its gross absence in most of the families studied in the district makes any fruit-bearing effective discussion worth the name possible embracing the pros and cons of the children's education and schooling.
- Alternatively poor socio-economic condition besides impeding any effective mediating role to reconcile the drop-outs with their unseen necessity for schooling, in a way acts a key-factor augmenting the conflict-ridden psychological state of the wards continuing schooling whereby even despite the keenness of the wards to regularly turn up for classes prevents them from doing so as the hostility-infected family atmosphere does not allow to any school apportioning of the family income for such schooling.
- It is thus to be painfully realised that is not only one controllable way poverty leads to drop-outs, but its many complex and intertwined natures of interference which may not be very effectively directly addressed even though the intensity of the challenge they pose could conceptually only measured.
- Studies consulted by this scholar as well as the present study conducted by him thoroughly bring out the

significance of the existing positive correlation among students' realised potential in terms of practical achievements in examinations, their motivational level and the problem of dropping out. It is understood that lower the satisfaction of individual students about their realised progress in studies, the lower the motivation level to continue schooling and thus, the higher the possibility of dropping out. Students' disenchantment with their self-progress in studies appears not to be in a condition of being improved within the existing nature of school administration and imparting of teaching because the present disenchantment level is a direct outcome of the present method, manner and mode of imparting education in the school. The remedy, arguably, could thus be located outside the presently defined school framework. Private home tuitions here are thought of as an immediate saving grace. But exorbitant costs of such private tuitions are even not things of dreams for the economically and socially backward tribal families whose immediate societies hardly have such examples to offer.

It is thus here to be seen that poverty is such a humbling and crushing force that this scholar is blank at mind thinking how to hold either the poorer parents on one hand or the subjects of drop-out themselves individually responsible for the problem of drop-outs that so glaringly faces us.

- When we talk of the present educational system and conclude that in its existing form it only is equipped best to aggravate the problem of drop-outs, an alternative vision remedying the present system to render it more responsive to tackle the said problem can only come through a service-minded mission-mode approach of the inspired teachers whose direct voluntary participation most probably can answer the necessity of private tuitions so as to ensure a constantly upward-looking realised confidence level of the students and thereby to arrest the problem. But in the present setup, such a noble and selfless service approach is a remote possibility as in the present day commodification of the education, teachers hardly find it in any way rewarding to go for such jobs in a society which is not very clear about the use of education itself. It could be seen that poor socio-economic condition of the people is responsible for lack of adequate teacher motivation to take up the job of service-teaching with any definite zeal where parents still are in need of upgradation of their awareness level about the profitability of education as an enterprise, it remains a challenge for even a few service-minded teachers to come out vigorously for any such bold and open agenda.

- Poor infrastructural arrangements at the school sites account for low levels of personal motivation for teachers to keep up normal routine teaching with frequent challenges to sustain a reasonably encouraging student attendance level through adequate motivational generation among students. Not being required to do the regular normal routine teaching mostly on account of a very low student attendance, teachers even with high qualifications posted in the interior schools do not undergo the necessity to update their knowledge. In estimable gap in time, it is naturally expected that such teachers will get far diminished in terms of intrinsic value in comparison of face value initially held up by their degrees.

Most primary schools in the interior areas of the district are locationally such disadvantageous that administration finds it impenetrable to have a regular supervisory control over the single-teacher-schools where irrespective of the disciplinary grooming the teachers are required to handle all subjects from Mathematics and Science to English and Social Studies. It remains here to be realised that a science student will be least interested in the arts subjects and an arts student will be least interested in the science subjects when asked to do the subjects in a single lot in the capacity of a teachers. Thus, disenchantment is inbuilt in the present system of education and its administration.

- Now it is time to posit our finding on what the drop-outs of various school-levels and age-groups do. In the foregoing observations we have noted that tempted by a consumerist culture, students experience the first bouts of dilemma as to whether to continue schooling in want and poverty or to discontinue studies to join the available labour-market. In most cases, the dilemma is resolved in favour of discontinuation of studies that leaves the drop-outs with ample of time at their disposal with which they could sell their labour to fulfil a few of their desires. It is however sadly to be pointed out that the illusion of earning a plentiful of income soon withers away and into the hard world of reality, they are compelled to get hurled with so saviour to rescue them. In the backward societies what next naturally comes to these crest fallen drop-outs is an early marriage with its subsequent early multiplication of the family that entails higher costs of maintenance which lower-income ranges many times fail to rise upto.

- It can be seen from what all is discussed above that poverty as a vicious circle continues to deal unbearable onslaughts to the drop-outs. The problem of the drop-outs emerges from the burning cauldron of abysmally low-levels of living engendered by poverty, misery and squalor; once the problem assumes shape, i.e. once drops out, one is incurably doomed to die in the perpetual cursed embrace of poverty. The problem of drop-outs is thus a very critical warning signal for the poor and backward tribal societies of Arunachal Pradesh, the inattention of which is bound to spell disaster for those societies individually in particular and the district and the state in the long run in general.

This is the helpless summary-finding of the present scholar that the problem of drop-outs needs urgent and deserved attention if the future of the indigenous Arunachalee tribal societies is to be secured against a total economic holocaust.

- The study being devoted to outlining the prospects of Higher Education in the district, it is a sad submission that despite unanimous scholastic emphasis on the indisputed all-round transformations to be rendered possible through an appropriate scheme of Higher Education in the district, the appealing figures of 56.49% of drop-outs at primary school education level, 75.9% at middle, 84.88% at secondary and 93.28% at post secondary school levels (figures averaged from the present study spread over 1994-95 to 1998-99) hold out little hope of higher education with a meagre 03 to 07 out of every hundred tribal boys and 02 to 05 out of every hundred tribal girls being found entering into the portals of higher educational institutions.
- Higher order jobs under the government, higher living standards and higher dreams for an ever upward-moving society being the fruits of higher education, with drop-out rates in this district being disturbingly so high, it remains only to be sadly predicted that until and unless the problem is very effectively and in reasonable time addressed, the tribal societies of this district will be bound to the chains of painful sub-standard living in the midst of grinding poverty, misery and squalor.
- *The scholar is deeply convinced that the drop-out problem is a major educational and social problem in this district. With parental illiteracy being as high as 83% (approx in the studied category) and the general drop-outs level being very high (as could be seen from the figures presented above), this assumes the proportion of being a very serious threat for the future social progress based on economic security. The journey*

of the district's tribes is apprehended to be that irretrievably from poverty to greater poverty through a sapping and unnerving sequence of grinding and abiding poverty. Hence, the following suggestions are submitted for the learned consideration of all concerned so that perhaps the lot of these hapless population of the state could be hopefully improved.

Suggestions

- In Arunachal Pradesh the department-wise planning is practised and the practice of linking manpower requirement with that of educational plans is missing. There is no coordination between the Department of Education and other departments, except the Department of Planning and Development which is responsible for formulation and execution of plans. It is therefore, suggested that like all other departments of the state, the Department of Education also plans independently taking into consideration its contributory role to the significant aspect of all-round transformation of the state to ably and proudly take its rightful place in the challenge-some new millennium that is very expectantly knocking at its door. It pre-supposes that a corrective perspective-illumined link be established among all departments where visibly education is made to assert its own status as the nucleus around which the rest of the state planning centres.

- The orientation of inspection and supervision has not been rendered responsive substantially. The common practice is to visit a school building and other physical facilities, inspect in a perfunctory manner its general functioning and evaluate it. To conduct surprise inspections either by ADEOs or AES OR DDSEs at the district level at regular intervals or by the state authorities at their convenience on the different educational institutions to ensure students' participation and involvement in the school activities is the need of the hour. The DDSE, even if , is over occupied with his official responsibility should find out time for such kind of inspection and supervision for a steady smooth and sound academic enrolment of an institution.

- Considering that the drop-out problem issues out basically from the inadequate and hazy functioning of the existing educational administrative machinery, effort should be effectively initiated so that vital dimensions like teacher's motivation, job satisfaction, organisational climate, effectiveness of teaching-learning process etc. are well taken care of an a committed administration springs into action and actual goals of education are achieved in terms of responsively linking the learner to the needs of his individual living and in making him substantially obliged to contribute towards achievement of the targeted transformational objectives of the society.

- There is a tremendous encouraging community zeal in realising a growing need for education of the upcoming generation in almost all the tribal societies in the district under study. What ails here, however, is the sad reality that these societies suffer from unimaginable levels of poverty that is mostly responsible for their all-round backwardness. Mere zeal does not sufficiently mean anything. What is required in the existing background is economically reasonably sufficiently self-sufficient they are rendered through appropriate government initiates whereunder people in order to fulfil their freshly discovered promises of education have to work, earn and save so that a new working sensible generation of educated young individuals comes into existence in close imitation of their hard pursuit of the transformational challenges thrown up by the new goals. Education verily is an encouraging device to help inculcate in the learners an ability to carve out individual destinies as successful struggle raisers, and for this if through proper examples a sustainable self-sufficient work-culture is developed, the drop-out problem could be addressed to a great extent.

- The institutional head who executes certain administrative and academic functions is also a sole factor on which they system of institutional development greatly depends. The way he uses these powers and the leadership he provides to his staff, are of crucial importance. The competence of heads of schools, therefore, needs to be properly assessed, and their leadership qualities identified, with regard to the specific demands and requirements of a particular school, before posting them. Heads should also be imparted specific orientation in techniques of planning and management of school, more particularly in the context of institutional planning as a toll of quality schooling.

- No doubt, the state government's programme of providing tribal children with textbooks and uniforms, simultaneously with the programme of 'mid-day meal' sponsored by the Central Government, has helped the system to retain them in the schools, but care must be taken by the administrators at different stages to see that the children are motivated to study too, and not just attend school only in the hope of a meal, books and uniforms. Moreover, the parents should not consider this free supply of meal, books and uniforms to their wards an expected financial benefit to the family income, saving a quarter part of their hard-earned money, but should take it a necessary prop to help render their wards a vigilance eye for the smooth maintenance of their schooling and studies.

In order to take corrective measures, the educational planners should first see that such children do not merely attend the school, but sufficient space is given in order to ensure that they also really come to the receiving point.

- Some schools do not have an adequate number of teachers, as subject teachers are not posted in time (most of the middle schools have 03 to 05 teachers in addition to a number of single teacher-managed primary schools in the village areas). Consequently, neither is the entire syllabus covered properly nor are the students prepared adequately for the examination. This leads to adoption of unfair means and low pass percentage in the Board of Examination conducted by CBSE. The posting of single teachers in the remote primary schools as discussed in our findings is a serious malady. The government as well as the district authorities should ensure that this kind of problem is eliminated.
- The government should also avoid posting of lady teachers and high qualified teachers in the remotest areas asking hours-together foot march which compels them either to absent themselves in the schools or to dilly-dally their responsible duties leading to the failure of the educational system as a whole. Moreover, the government should notice to it that only trained teachers are recruited, most specifically for English and Mathematics to develop a better teaching standard in the given class room environment and to facilitate in service untrained teachers to go for training courses at least once or twice in their service period with government-sponsored expenses and leave. The government should also not sit silent with this kind of attempt. It is further to ensure that these in service teachers after getting themselves trained, get adequate incentives to encourage his lazy and disinterested fellow friends to go for such training. The teachers, on the other hand, should utilise their trained potentialities on the classroom dynamics generating interests among the students to come regularly to the classes and to avoid drop-out.
- The transfer and posting of teachers in the mid-session has been a great problem cited by most of the teachers

questioned under the field survey. Mention may be made that this kind of problem places the teachers, students and the institutions into difficulty. The kind of educational atmosphere that an institution renders to the students, the kind of teaching method that a teacher develops inside the class on a particular topic, the kind of target he fixes to finish the syllabus and the kind of learning-mentality that a student fosters in himself in the given class room surroundings, all cease to exist with the transfer of a teacher in the mid-session. And it takes time to notice experience the same kind of environment to go with all of them, the teacher, the student and the institution. But the period-inter-regnum is hardly compensated. The loss of the period becomes a permanent loss for all of them. Hence, the government being a part and parcel of the whole educational system should realise it as lapse on its part and make it a policy to stop effecting this practice.

- To improve the quality of education and maintain sufficient essential facilities like posting at least two teachers in each primary school, constructing two class rooms under RLEGP school providing games and sports materials and playgrounds, organising school games and other extra-curricular activities, allocating annual fund for library purchasing, providing audio-visual sets as far as possible and above all, providing the educational institutions adequate good quality study materials, the government should take up adequate measures. Moreover, it should initiate the plan to organise educational programmes or exhibitions in the village/circle area to arouse consciousness among the students and their parents to develop new orientation towards education. Opening communication facilities around the schools particularly in the rural areas would prove to be a necessary boon in this respect which would remove the feeling of remoteness and exclusion from the minds of the students' encourage them to feel updated comparatively and intensify their interests to regularly come to school.

- The greatest malady encouraging the problem of drop out and thwarting the smooth progress of education in the district has been the early marriage and early parenthood of the school-goers as found by the scholars in the village areas during his field study. Most of the parents when asked about the reasons for their ward's dropping out, have cited 'early marriage' as an important factor. Early marriage taking place at the school going age contributes adversely to the academic progress and achievement of the couple concerned. Besides, existing social taboos pertaining to married women's social behaviour create a lot of hindrance and girl-child education gets squeezed in scope. Early production and early parenthood with their attendant responsibilities and financial liabilities make even the male-partner, who can pursue his studies conveniently, mad and subsequently demotivated. The result is that the mother to attend to the baby-care necessities naturally becomes a drop-out whereas circumstantial compositions make the father (the student) also an eventual drop-out. If through this problem a substantial channel of the progress of education is blocked it is the responsibility of the government to see to it that the problem stands eliminated.

- The issue which needs immediate care and attention is the high incidence of drop out at the several stages of education specifically at the elementary stage. The retention of children in schools is an important element of universalisation of elementary education (UEE). The state provides free text books, stationery and uniforms to children at the primary stage in addition to the scheme of 'mid-day meal' sponsored by the Central Government. Since the state is basically a tribal one, it should explore special facilities and programmes which exist under the tribal sub-plan. It is to be ensured that special projects are formulated on micro level to increase retention of children in schools and reduce drop out rates. Community involvement may be of great benefit in checking the rate of drop-out.

In the all India perspective when the drop-out problem already assumes a highly gnawing proportion, in the North Eastern context, in Arunachal Pradesh context and most specifically in the context of West Kameng District, this problem stands out clearly as some such significantly attention-engaging malady that is bound to upset all the goals of social transformation and of development of any name in its callous neglect. Education uncontestedly is the prime mover and stabiliser and pace-setter of any developmental undertaking. Educational proliferation as a neatly throughout scheme to usher in the scintillating era of all-round development gets a major set-back with drop-out problem eating into its vitals. The planners of development in all sectors will have to take care to ensure that through a consensual approach the government is rendered convinced to allocate its deserved priority to education in matters of funds allotment so that the past folly perpetrated in ignorance of making education the first casualty whenever a serious resource crunch is to be addressed, is not repeated in future. Out deepest concern and sincerest problem into the drop-out issue leave us enlightened as to how by empowering the parents in the economically backward communities the like of whom people our survey in this district we can plug the drop-out problem in the most succinct manner. Early marriage as well come to understand is also accepted and encouraged by the economically backward sections of the tribal communities of the district mostly because marriage of the son means addition of a working and earning hand into the family pool of active labour-force. Though soon the disillusion sets in, it does not serve as an eye opener to the rest in a community when as at different points of time and to different magnitudes families stand exposed in terms of sufferings.

All through our observations we have resolutely confirmed our apprehensions that poverty is at the back of the mischief of drop-out from the educational net. Composite development planning in our studied stand can never afford to ignore the wisdom of endorsing the top priority that education of the younger generations is bound to enjoy in a healthy and pragmatically thinking society.

It is our humblest submission that the government at all levels gets to know its role to move in the suggested right direction of setting up resource-pools on the basis of a wisely chalked out composite development plan and in all sincerity of purposes implements the educational advancement scheme with a strict eye on the drop-out issue.

APPENDIX

Questionnaire-I

1. Student's Profile

Name	*Sex*	*Age*	*Tribe/ Caste*	*Village/Town Permanent Present*	*Connected with roads Pucca Kutcha*	*Distance from Dist. Hq. /C. O. Hq.*

2. Educational History of the Student

Name of the School	*Year in which took admission*	*Age at the of time admission*	*Classes in which he studied*	*Class from which he dropped out*	*Total years in school*	*Remarks*

3. Post-dropout Details of the Student

Present Occupation	*If employed*		*If works with family*		*Other details (Unemployed etc.)*
	Nature of Job	*Income per day/month*	*Nature of work*	*No. of manday*	

4. Family Background

Sl. No.	*Name(s)*	*Sex*	*Age*	*Relationship with student*	*Primary occupation*	*Income Per month*	*Educational qualification*	*Other information*
Head the of Household								
Others 2. 3. 4. 5.								
Total						Total Income		

5. Economic Data of the Family/Household

Total land owned/ Operated		Type of House	No. of rooms	Total sq. feet approx.	Homestead land area	Assets movable	Total Income		
Individually	Share from the collective pulls						From agri.	From other sources	Total

6. Access to Modern Facilities/Media Exposure

Type of facility	*Available *(put a tick mark)	*Not Available	Details of Accessibility
1. Electricity			
2. Newspaper			
3. Radio			
4. T.V.			
5. Clock			
6. Audio-sets			
7. Video-sets			

7. Questions to Parents/Guardians

a) Name of the Respondant/Parents-

b) Why did your son/daughter discontinue from school? Details

Ans: (i) Failure in Exam ______
(ii) Financial problems ______
(iii) Health problems ______
(iv) Problems related to school ______
(v) Others ______

c) Do you think going to school is good for a child? -Yes- -No-

d) Did your try to send your ward back to school? -Yes- -No-

e) Is he obedient/well behaved? -Yes- -No-

f) Was he happier when he used to go to the school? -Yes- -No-

g) What do you think about his future?

______

h) If Illiterate, what are the problems you are facing in the recent days?

______

i) Do you think that education has got a value in the society?

______

Questionnaire-II

Questions to the Students

1. Why did you stop going to school?
2. How was your school?
   - very good
   - good
   - neither good nor bad
   - bad
3. Did you enjoy studying?
   - Yes – No
4. What do you think about your teachers?
   - all/most of them were good
   - all/most of them were bad
   - some of them were nice
   - only a few were good, others bad
   - none of them was good
5. Do you remember them?
   - Yes – No
6. Who was your favourite teacher (Name)?
7. Why was he favourite?
   - He was teaching well
   - He never beat me
   - He was helping in nature
   - He did not bother about the classes
8. Were you ever beaten up by your teacher?
   - regularly
   - quite often

– once in a while

– never

9. Did you have good friends in the school?

– Yes – No

10. Can you name them?

_______________ The friends

_______________ a) belong to the same locality

– Yes – No

_______________ b) belong to the same caste/tribe

– Yes – No

11. Do you meet/play with them even after you stopped going to school?

– Yes – No

12. Do you think the school days were better?

– Yes – No

13. Why? ______________________________

____

14. Would you like to go to the school once again, if you were given a chance?

– Yes – No

15. Did you find the curriculum very tough?

– Yes – No

16. Which of the subjects were

a) most difficult ______________________________

b) easier ______________________________

17. Apart from studies, what interests you most?

____

18. Did you get a chance to take part in your school ?

– games

- cultural activities
- litercy activities

19. Whom do you envy much in your village (Name)? ____________________

20. And why?
    - rich/wealthy having vehicles
    - educated and intelligent
    - powerful (gaonburah/ASM/ Public leader/MLA
    - dominating in nature
    - strong
    - employed earning much
    - any other traditionaly influential

21. What attracts you more when you visit any town or city?
    - crowd
    - beautiful garments
    - beautiful cosmetics
    - motor cycles/cars/gypsies etc.
    - palatable dishes in the restaurant
    - electronic goods
    - tambola/dice
    - others, if any

22. What do you like to purchase when you visit any town or city even if you do not have money ?
    - beautiful garments
    - beautiful cosmetics
    - vehicles
    - palatable dishes in the restaurant
    - electronic goods
    - others, if any

23. How do your teacher make you understand the subject?

    – by clarifying in English only
    – in Hindi only
    – in Assamese only
    – in both Assamese and Hindi only
    – in both Assamese and English only
    – in both English and Hindi only

24. How was your Principal/Headmaster-Teacher relationship ?

    – good
    – bad
    – average
    – extremely good

Questionnaire-III

Questions to the Teachers

1. Teacher's Bio-Data

Name	*Age*	*Sex*	*Educational Qualifications*	*Special Training*	*State of Domicile*	*Years of Service*	
						Total	*In the Present Institution*

Gross pay per month	Family members to be supported	Govt. accomo-dation available		No. of rooms	Total hours spent weekly		
		Pucca	Kutcha		Taking classes	Official duties	Personal work

2. What is your idea about students in your school?
   - Most of them are good students
   - Most of them are bad students
   - Most of them are average students
3. Give reasons:
   - ________________________
   - ________________________
   - ________________________
4. Do you think the students find it interesting to come to school?

   – Yes – No
5. Reasons:

   ____

6. Do you think the syllabus is very tough/easy/alright?
7. What is the most difficult subject to be taught and why?

   Ans. ______________________________

8. In which subject you find your students to be least interested and why?

   Ans. ______________________________

9. Do you think the method of teaching you adopt is all right?

   – Yes – No

10. If yes, Why?

    ____

11. Do you think any improvement is necessary for better teaching standards?

    ____

12. What are the main reasons behind the students dropping out?

    ____

    ____

    ____

13. Are you happy with your life?

    – Yes – No

14. Do you think the society pays respect to you as a teacher?

    – Yes – No

15. Would you like your ward to be a teacher?

    – Yes – No

16. Why? Reasons:

    ____

17. What are the problems faced by you as a teacher?

____

____

____

18. Are you satisfied with the infrastructure of the school in comparison to the students strength?

– Yes – No

19. What are the shortcomings?

____

____

____

20. Have you ever insisted the students to drop out?

– Yes – No

21. If No, Why? Reasons:

If Yes, what response have you got?

____

____

____

22. Have you ever insisted the parents to send their wards back to school even after dropped out?

– Yes – No

23. If No, Why? Reasons:

If Yes, what response have you got?

____

____

____

24. How is Goanburah?

– very co-operative
– non co-operative
– indifferent
– average

BIBLIOGRAPHY

Arora, G.L. (1984) (ed.): *Reflections on Curriculum* , NCERT, New Delhi.

Barro, S. (1984), *The Incidence of Dropping Out: A Descriptive Analysis,* Washington DC: Economic Research.

Blaug, M. (1970), *An Introduction to Economics of Education,* Allen Lane, Penguin, London.

Berli, Updesh K. (1990) (ed.), *Researchers in Child Development* (NCERT).

Bickel, R. and S. Milton (1983), "The Social Circumstances of Illiteracy", *Urban Review* 15: 203-15.

Census of India (1991): Series 1, Paper 1 of 1991.

Census of India (1992): Final Population Totals, Paper 2 of 1992.

Coleman, J. (1961), *The Adoloscent Society,* New York: Free Press.

D'Amico, R (1984), "Does Employment During High School Impair Academic Progress?", *Sociology of Education* 57: 152-64.

Department of Education, Ministry of Human Resource Development, Government of India, *Education in India,* Volume-I, 1975-76, Volume-I, 1980-81, Volume I, 1985-86, *Selected Educational Statistics,* 1990-91, 1992.

Duncan, B. (1965), "Dropouts and the Unemployed," *Journal of Political Economy* 73: 121-34.

Durkheim, E. (1951): *Suicide,* Glencoe, Ill: Free Press.

Dutt, Rudar (1996), "Inequalities in Educational Development, With Special Reference to Literacy Status and School Education", *Journal of Educational Planning and Administration (JEPA),* Vol. X, No. 3, July, NIEPA, New Delhi.

EPW-Economic and Political Weekly (April 26-May 2 1997): Vol. XXXII No. 17: Bombay.

Five Year Plan, Third (1961): New Delhi.

Ghosh, Arun (1992), *Planning in India: The Challenges for the Nineties*: New Delhi.

Greenberger, E. and L. Steinberg (1986), *When Teenagers Work: The Psychological and Social Costs of Adolescent Employment,* New York.

Grover, B.L. (1984), *A New Look on Modern Indian History,* New Delhi.

Heyneman, S. and Loxley, W. (1982), "Influences on Academic Achievement Across High and Low Income Countries: A Re-analysis of IEA Data", *Sociology of Education,* Washington, 55(1), January: 13-21.

Heyneman, S. And Loxley, W. (1983), "The Effect of Primary School Quality on Academic Achievement Across Twenty Nine High and Low Income Countries", *American Journal of Sociology,* Washington, 88(6): 1162-64.

Hirschi, T. (1969), *Causes of Delinquency,* Berkeley: University of California Press.

Hossler, D., Lund, J.P., Ramin, J., Wesfall, S. and Irish, S. (1997), "State Funding for Higher Education: The Sisyphean Task", *The Journal of Higher Education,* Ohio

State University Press, Columbia, 68(2), March/April: 160-190.

Joseph, K.S. (1997), "Classroom Language and Effective Communication", *Journal of the Society for Educational Research and Development*, Vol. 13, No. 3, July, Baroda.

Journal of Educational Planning and Administration, NIEPA, New Delhi, Vol. X, No. 3, July, 1996; Vol. XII, No. 1, January, No.2, April, No. 3, July and No. 4, October, 1998.

Kapoor, N.M., R.P. Vadhera and Srilekha Majumdar (1995), *Educational Administration in Arunachal Pradesh*, NIEPA, New Delhi.

Kingdon, Geeta Gandhi (1998), "How Much do Schools Matter to Pupil Achievement in India?" *The Journal of EPA*, NIEPA, New Delhi, XII(I), January: 17-18.

Lakshmi, S. (1992): Innovations in Education: New Delhi, Lewin-Epstein, N. (1981): *Youth Employment During High School*, Washington DC: National Center for Education Statistics.

Magnusson, Jamie-Lynn (1997), *Higher Education Research and Psychological Inquiry*, Ohio State University Press, Columbia 68(2), March/April: 191-211.

Majumdar, R.C. (1954), *History and Culture of Indian People*, Bombay.

Manning, W. (1990), "Parenting Employed Teenagers." *Youth and Society* 22: 184:-200.

Mathew, E.T. (1996), 'Financial Aspects of Privatisaton of Higher Education: Issues and Opinions', *EPW* (April-6), Vol. XXXI, No. 14, Bombay.

McNeal R. (1995), "Extracurricular Activities and High School Drop-outs", *Sociology of Education* 68, 62-81.

Mookherjee, R.K. (1938), *Ancient Indian Culture*, London.

Naik, J.P. (1978), *'Education' Commissions and After,* New Delhi.

______ (1958), *Educational Planning in India,* Bombay.

Nath, Prem (1990), *The Bases of Education,* New Delhi.

Naik J.P. and Nurullah, S.(1951), *A History of Education in India,* Bombay.

National Council of Educational Research and Training (NCERT) (1992), *Fifth All India Educational Survey,* New Delhi.

Papagiannis, G., R. Bickel, and R. Fuller (1983), "The Social Creation of School Dropouts." *Youth and Society* 14: 363-92.

Phillips. S. and K. Sandstrom, 1990, "Parental Attitudes Toward Youth Work." *Youth and Society* 21 : 168-83.

Post-war Educational Development (1944), New Delhi.

Powar, K.B. (1997), *Higher Education in India Since Independence: Respect and Future Options,* AMU Occassional Paper 97/1

Raina, B.L. (1992), *Education and Development*: Ambala.

Ralph, B. McNeal (Jr.) (1997), "Are Students being Pulled out of High School? The Effect of Adolescent Employment on Dropping Out", *Journal of the Sociology of Education,* Washington, 70(3), July: 206-220.

Rao, I.V Chalapati (1992), *College Teachers and Administrators, A Handbook,* Hyderabad.

Report of the Universtiy Education Commission (1950): Vol. 1.

Report Annual (1994-95): Department of Education, Government of India.

Registrar General of India (1997): R.G.I. Letter No. 6-3/95 DD Vol. II dated 24.6.1997. (1996): S

Selected Educational Statistics, 1991-92.

Sidhanta Rajana, 'Education' in V.B. Singh (ed.) *Economic History of India.*

Singh, Amrik (1997), 'The Place of Secondary Education', *Economic and Political Weekly* (April 26-May 2): Vol. XXXII. No. 17, Bombay.

Singh, Inderpal (1996) (ed.), *School Education: Some Reflections*, New Delhi.

Subrahmanyam, S. (1984), "The Relative Influence of Home and School on Reading Achievement in Primary School Children", *Journal of Education and Psychology*, 42(3) (October).

Sixth All India Educational Survey (1998), *National Tables* Vol. I *(Schools and Physical Facilities)* and Vol. II *(Teachers in Schools)* NCERT, New Delhi.

Teacher Education in Arunachal Pradesh, National Council of Teacher Education, New Delhi, 1998.

Tilak, J.B.G. (1997), 'Five Decades of Underinvestment in Education', *EPW* (September 6-12), Vol. XXXII, No. 36, Bombay.

Trends of Drop-out Rates for years 1980-81 to 1993-94 (1995): Ministry of Human Resource Development, Department of Education, Planning, Monitoring and Statistics Division, New Delhi.

Universtiy Education in India (1956), Government of India, Publications Division.

INDEX

A

AICSE, 21

AIES, 206

All India Council for Technical Education, 27

Arora, G.L., 59

Arunachal Pradesh, overview of its education system, 79-127
- curriculum and syllabi, 111
- educational institutions, 83
- educational system, 80
  - literacy, 80
  - structure, 81
- educational planning, 109
- elementary education, 98
- expansion of school education during 9th plan, 118
- future perspectives, 116
- history of education department, 94
- inspection and supervision, 115
- pay scales, 105
- school textbooks, 110
- secondary education, 100
- selection and recruitment, 101
  - of teachers, 102
  - posting and transfer, 103
- special features of, 80
- state level setup, 101
- students' evaluation, 113

B

Barro, 200

Bickel, 198, 200

BIMARU state, 8

Blaug, 41

C

Calcutta University Commission, 19

Chalapathi Rao, 71

Coleman, 198

Curriculum design, 73

D

D'Amico, 200

Directive Principles of State Policy, 17

Dropout rates, 47

Duncan, 200

E

ECCE, 24

Education Commission, 22, 64

Education in India (higher), growth of, 17
- post-Independence

development, 19

Education,
- essence and role of, 3
- props for development, 15-51
- SC/ST enrolment, 45

EFA goal, 9

Elementary education, 31

EPW, 21, 22, 31, 39

F

Five Year Plan,
- education outlay in, 28

Fuller, 198

G

Ghosh, Arun, 16

Greenberger, 199

Grover, B.L., 23

Growth of literacy,
- and gender inequalities, 41

H

Higher Education, 38

K

Kapoor, 80

Kothari Commission, 21, 65

L

Lakshmi, S., 23

Lewin-Epstein, 198

Literacy,
- growth of, 41
- low level literacy, 47
- rate of SC and ST, 45
- regional scenario, 43

Local inhabitants,
- Aka, 132
- Khawa, 134
- Miji (Dhammai), 131
- Monpas, 130
- Sherdukpen, 133

M

Majumdar, R.C., 17

Manning, 198

Mathew, E.T., 39

Mazumdar, 80

McNeal, 200

Middle schools, 120
- teachers, 122

Milton, 198, 200

Mookherjee, R.K., 17

Mudaliar, A.L., 20

N

Nagpaul, Hans, 21

Naik, J.P., 7, 18, 19

Nath, 57

Nath, Prem, 10

National Policy on Education (1980), 23

National Policy on Education, 95

Navodaya Vidyalayas, 25

NCERT, 21, 34, 87, 111, 112

NFE, 25

North-Eastern Areas (Reorganisation) Act of 1972, 79

Nurullah, S., 18

O

Operation Blackboards, 25, 119

P

Papagiannis, 198

Phillips, 198

PMOST, 88

Practical method, 76

Present study,
- epilogue, 204, 226
- introduction, 1
- objectives, 12

methodology, 12
significance, 13
tools, 13
Privatisation, 39
Problem and critical eye, 174-203

R

Rani, B.L., 7
Rao, 75
Reading techniques, 69
Refresher courses, 68

S

Sandstorm, 198
Secondary Education Commission, 20
Secondary education, 34
Sergeant Report, 19
Sindhanta, Ranjana, 18
Singh, Inderpal, 4, 64
Steinberg, 198, 199

T

Teacher and value inculcation, 64
Teacher education, strengthening, 125
Teaching and testing, dynamics of, 52-78
Teaching methods,
bulletin boards, 59
chalk board, 60
computer, 63
curriculum, 56
face-to-face contacts, 55
flimstrip projector, 61
overhead projector, 60
radio, 62
right information, 54
side projector, 61
tape recorder, 62
television, 63
Textbooks and instructional materials,
provision of, 124
Theoretical method, 74

U

UEE, 89, 204
UNESCO, 9, 15, 16
Universal Declaration of Human Rights, 16
University Education Commission, 18, 20
University Grants Commission, 20

V

Vadhera, 80

W

West Kameng district, 128-173
administrative setup, 135
climate, 129
education, 139
highlights of important aspects of, 136-139
historical genesis, 128
local inhabitants, 130
lower level organisation setup, 140
physiography, 129
population, 130
role of local bodies, 142
Woods Despatch, 18

Z

Zakir Hussain, 59

❑❑❑